Wild Running

Wild Running

South Wales

Natalie Ann Holborow

Seren Books is the book imprint of
Poetry Wales Press Ltd
Derwen Road, Bridgend, Wales
www.serenbooks.com

Find us on social media @SerenBooks

© Natalie Ann Holborow, 2025
Photography © Ceri Llewellyn

The right of Natalie Ann Holborow to be identified
as the authors of this work has been asserted
in accordance with the Copyright,
Designs and Patents Act, 1988.

ISBN 978-1-78172-787-4

A CIP record for this title is available
from the British Library.

All rights reserved. No part of this publication may be reproduced, stored in
a retrieval system, or transmitted at any time or by any means electronic,
mechanical, photocopying, recording or otherwise without the prior
permission of the copyright holders.

The publisher works with the financial assistance of the
Books Council of Wales.

No part of this book may be used or reproduced in any manner
for the purpose of training artificial intelligence technologies or systems.

The publisher works with the financial assistance
of the Books Council of Wales.
EU GPSR Authorised Representative
Logos Europe, 9 rue Nicolas Poussin, 17000,
La Rochelle, France
E-mail: Contact@logoseurope.eu

Cover by Seren Books

Printed by 4Edge, Hockley.

Contents

Introduction	7
Oxwich Bay	11
Parkmill and Three Cliffs	29
Castell Coch	43
Caerphilly Mountain	55
Brombil Reservoir	69
Pen-y-Fan	81
Ogmore-by-Sea	95
Merthyr Mawr	109
Salmon Leaps	123
Cefn Bryn	137
Llantwit Major	153
Pen Pych	165
Tintern Abbey	179
Llanrhidian	191
Notes	204
Acknowledgements	206
About the Author	208

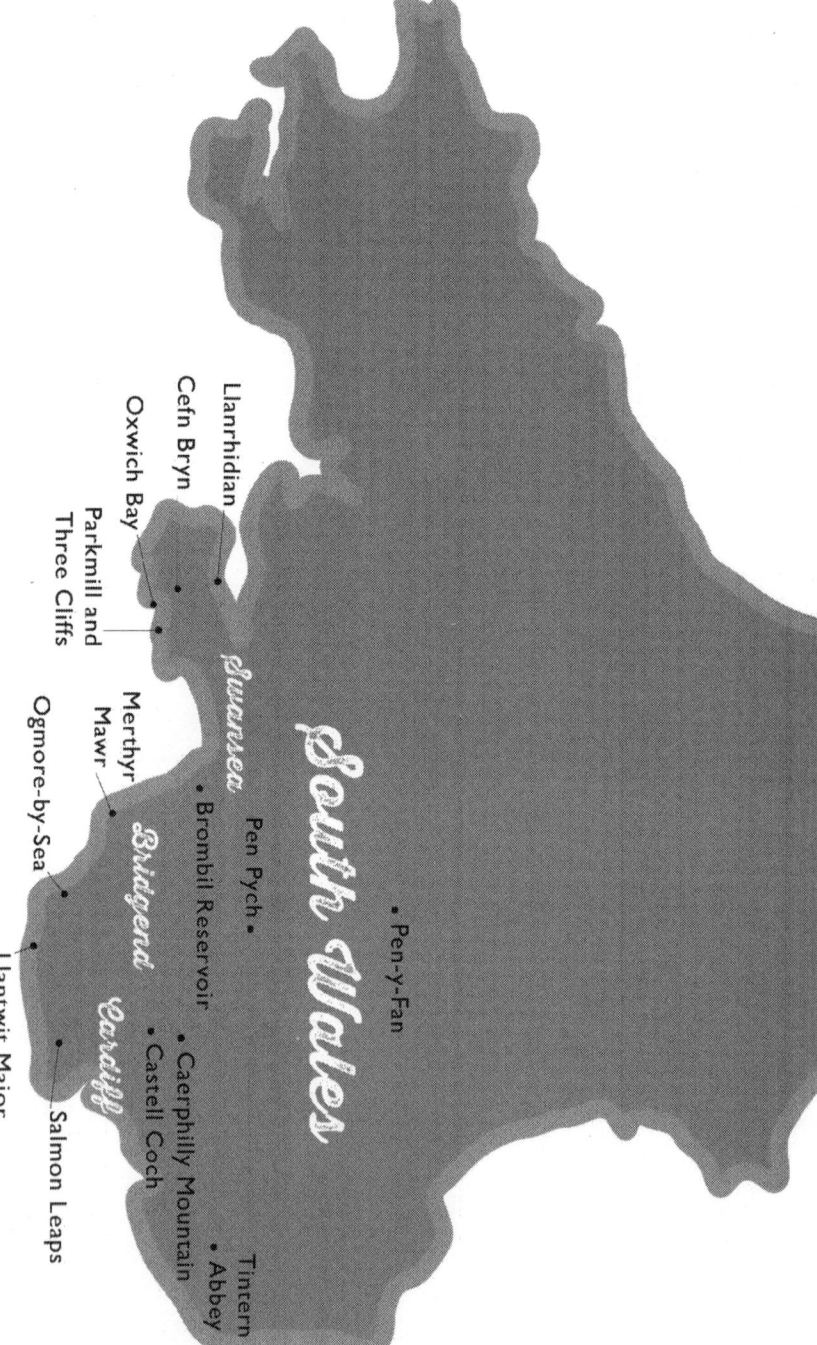

Introduction

While writing this book, I was asked, "What *is* wild running?" And, to be honest, I couldn't answer. I'd assumed it meant trail running, or at least some sort of run that involved brambles, thick mud, or feral animals.

I like to think of wild running as an act of remembering why you run. It's about being in your body, in a place, at a pace that allows noticing, for example, the way light filters through pine, or the moment a heron lifts into flight as you round the bend. It's less about speed or stats, and more about connection, rhythm, and presence.

Sometimes, it's a meditation. Sometimes, it's a mess. Often, it's both (as I'll prove in this book).

Wild running, I have come to decide, is running as a natural instinct.

This book came to life as part running diary, part love letter to South Wales, part poetic detour through mud, moss, myth, and malfunctioning sports bras. And, most importantly, it was born through connection.

You won't find advice on how to get a sub-3 marathon (God, I can't manage one of those). You won't find a list of supplements that promise to make you run like an Olympian or an in-depth analysis of VO2 max (because, honestly, I can't be bothered). What you will find are stories, from myself and from the wonderful people who've accompanied me. In writing this book, I've been fascinated by how running connects us to ourselves, to each other, and to the world around us.

These routes are not always the neatest or the flattest. They are not PR-chasers. They are runs that make you slow down;

sometimes for the views, but often because you're ankle-deep in manure. Don't worry, I promise you'll get used to it.

In slowing down, I found something important: that running these wild parts of South Wales invites you to really notice things and not just sleepwalk through the route. To run, but also to look, listen, and notice how the light melts upon the moss in late spring. How garlic flowers unfurl like origami stars in May. How a ruined abbey can look like a cathedral of ghosts when the morning mist is dense enough.

The routes in this book range from the sweeping cliffs of Gower to the shaded woods around Tintern, from sun-bleached sand dunes to the rocky outcrops of Pen Pych. Each run is different, but all of them invite you to do the same thing: to come and see what happens when you let an unpredictable landscape set the pace.

I'm not a running coach or a top athlete. I'm a writer. And what I've learned from running these trails is that the act of putting one foot in front of the other (particularly when you really don't want to) has a magic all of its own. These runs pulled me out of creative ruts. They helped me process grief. They've helped me cope with mounting stress. They reminded me of how much beauty we have right on our doorstep in South Wales, and how we so often overlook it in favour of ticking off the next destination with a filter-ready backdrop for our social media feeds.

Sometimes I write mid-run. Sometimes I just hold the lines in my head and hope they survive the descent. Sometimes the run itself is the poem. That sounds like an excuse, I know, but it's not.

This book doesn't ask that you're an elite runner or even particularly fit. It's for those who run to feel something shift inside them, even if it's only the weight of a bad day dropping from the shoulders. It's for the reluctant joggers and the messy, breathless triers. It's for the ones who run to feel their body come alive again, even if it's wheezing and tripping over itself far too often.

Introduction

And most of all, it's for the ones who love wild places.

Each chapter will take you through a different trail in South Wales, from the industrial bones of Tintern's Wireworks Bridge to the soft belly of Llanrhidian Marsh. You'll find historical snippets, folklore tangents, and more than a few interludes where I panic about cows. I'll tell you where the best coffee is, which climbs are secretly awful, and what to avoid if you're wearing white shoes (basically, nearly everything).

This book isn't just mine. Many of these routes were gifted to me: recommended by friends, fellow runners, readers, and kind strangers online. Some were offered with a reverent sort of pride, others with a cheery warning ('You'll hate me for the hill, but the view is worth it!'). Every single one became part of this slow, unravelling journey through the places I thought I knew, but didn't really, until I ran them.

Maybe it'll be a fox, blurring like a firework across an urban path. Maybe it'll be a cluster of bluebells, rinsing the woodland floor in a wash of lilacy-blue. Maybe it'll be a line of dialogue you've been trying to crack for days. Or maybe it'll be the sudden realisation that your body, however much it aches, is still capable of movement and little wins you'll probably only keep to yourself. Or, of course, your Strava followers.

Or, you know, maybe it'll just be a really good slab of carrot cake at the end of a 10K.

Whatever it is, I hope these runs bring you something. Perhaps a deep breath of air in the lungs when you didn't realise how long you'd been holding it.

If nothing else, I promise you'll at least know exactly where the best tearooms are in case it all goes sideways. Happy running.

Oxwich Bay

Location
Oxwich Bay
SS 501865

Distance
Approx. 5K

Parking
Oxwich Bay Car Park (bring coins unless you like awkwardly searching your pocket for loose change while people huff behind you).

Facilities
Toilets, food, drink, and post-run relief at the Oxwich Bay Hotel or The Dunes Café. Also public toilets near the beach, which is always reassuring to know.

Tips
Bring water and a sense of humility for the uphill climb. Wear trail shoes for grip, especially if it's rained recently.

Oxwich Bay

Oxwich Bay is one of those places that always looks subtly beautiful, no matter how grumpy you are (which, today, I am). The waves heave in like smelted iron, its cliffs overlapping themselves like drunkenly assembled shelves, its trees in the autumn crowned with a glorious copper.

Getting there is scenic enough to lift my mood, if only briefly. We drive through Swansea, past chain stores and the usual heavy summer traffic, then head towards Mumbles. We resist being pulled in the direction of Verdi's café, where couples are queuing for cappuccinos they'll post to their Instagram feeds but never finish before they get cold. As we reach Blackpill, we take the turn towards Mayals and let the road carry us up and over onto the Gower Peninsula.

The air through the open window is a little different here. It's cooler, saltier, and after last week's rainfall it's just a refreshing amount of damp. In summer, I'll often catch the sweet tang of garlic as I dip through Parkmill, the roadsides thick with foliage. Just as we're starting to relax, the descent begins – a winding plunge towards Oxwich Bay that feels less like a road and more like a budget rollercoaster.

By the time we arrive at Oxwich, my GPS is struggling to find itself (aren't we all), but I don't care. The bay sprawls out ahead, the tide breathing slow and deliberate. On this particular September morning, the light hangs low and moody, turning everything into a sun-bleached watercolour. Dogs zigzag across the beach, tails slicing the air like helicopter blades. Nearby, shivering wild swimmers emerge from the sea, their faces a chattering mix of triumph and hypothermia.

In the summer months, unless you are early, the queues for

the beach car park stretch most of the way along the hill. By autumn it's quieter, but you're still going to need coins for the car park attendant. No days off for him.

I scrabble in the cup holder, clinking out twenty-pence pieces while the attendant watches me with remarkable patience.

Ian, my partner, looks effortlessly prepared as usual. His running jacket is zipped tight, and he's stretched precisely none of the muscles he's about to use. It's all a performance, or at least that's what I think anyway, balancing on one leg doing a half-hearted hamstring stretch. Meanwhile, Ted, our Jack Russell Terrier, is already bouncing on his lead like he's just downed three espressos and not half a tin of Butcher's chicken with rice and peas.

Today I've woken up in a terrible mood. I've been trying to finish the edits for my latest poetry book for weeks, but the writing is coming to me stubbornly. Every edit falls flat and I simply don't have time for this sort of creative block right now. I figured a run would help, but now that I'm here, facing the slate-coloured waves slumping against the shore, I'm unconvinced.

I zip my jacket up as far as it will go without cutting off circulation to my head. Time to get on with it.

We start just outside the Oxwich Bay Hotel. Outdoor tables cluster under bright, optimistic parasols, despite the bloated clouds and damp air. Inside, figures in rain-prickled coats and with windswept hair huddle over steaming mugs, their conversations punctuated by the clink of forks against plates loaded with monumental slabs of carrot cake. My resolve wavers. Grumpy and hormonal, I long to sink into one of those chairs and warm my hands on a coffee mug instead but Ian is already pushing on ahead, his stride measured and determined, while Ted is a reddish blur of energy, trampling everything in his wake.

I click my Garmin to "run" mode and force my legs to keep moving. I have no idea if my creative muse will be running with me today. After 16 years of being a writer, I still have no idea what platitudes are the right ones to whisper to coax it out.

The path past the hotel starts flat, which is perfect for warming up. My advice is to go slower than you intended here, no matter how full of energy you're feeling. Every ounce of that energy will be needed shortly. After a few minutes of gently meandering trail, the path tips upward. First, it's a gradual slope. Manageable, I'd say. Then it becomes something else: Oxwich's endless steps – a hellish ascent carved into the hillside by, I presume, the Devil himself. Uneven and slick with moss, the steps rise seemingly without an end point, testing my mental strength as much as my cardiovascular fitness. My confidence evaporates within minutes.

Ian and Ted are dots ahead of me, Ian pacing with infuriating calm, Ted bounding weightlessly as though he's pouncing over the moon.

Just when I think I'm nearing the top, a new flight of steps seems to emerge from nowhere. Whoever built them overestimated the stamina of a typical human. Anyway, I am here, halfway to peak fitness or total defeat, staring at the old stone of St. Illtyd's Church below me.

St. Illtyd's wasn't always a church. Long before twelfth-century architects got to work on it, this ancient hill was sacred. The story goes that Saint Illtyd, a wandering monastic Celt (he'll pop up a few times in this book), set up a small cell here in the 6th century. By the twelfth century, the cell had grown into a proper church, complete with a nave and a western tower. Over the years the building gained some flourishes, and by the fourteenth century there were Gothic battlements, a Norman arch, and a bell inscribed with the words *Sancta Maria, ora pro nobis* (Holy Mary, pray for us).[1] Sometimes, you might hear that bell still clanging for attention, eerie over the rushing waves.

Inside the church (we won't be going in today, but if you do, you might want to know a little more about it), there's a chancel with effigies: Sir John Penrice and his wife Margaret

Fleming, posing in alabaster as if they're standing there for a medieval family portrait. Historians say they lived here during the fourteenth century, and their stony repose is either a testament to their wealth or just exhaustion from centuries of people mispronouncing their names.

If you're also a fan of the supernatural, I can't recommend highly enough a visit to the grounds of St Illtyd's, which are reputed to be haunted by the *ceffyl dŵr*, a ghostly water horse from Welsh folklore, said to slip into the dried-up depths. In the late Victorian age, the Rev'd John David Davies recalled how his older brother was out fishing with their father in the sea below. As night fell and they made their way back up to the rectory, he had a strange feeling of being followed. He looked back and saw "a white horse walking on its hind legs" and drifting towards the church.[2] Sightings have been reported since.

Halfway up those steps, out of breath and slightly light-headed, I thought I saw something flicker just beyond the gravestones – but then again, there's a 99% chance it was Ted propelling himself in furious pursuit of a leaf.

Wheezing, I stop and tap at my phone:

> *The gravestones lean like tipsy scholars, their names salt-smudged…somewhere beyond them, the sea is busy reminding itself how to let go of breath.*

Maybe this sudden line will never go anywhere and I'll cringe at it tomorrow, but it's a start at least.

*

Finally, I reach the summit of the steps. I look down at the tipsy trail below me to see an older couple meandering back down with their hiking poles without breaking a sweat.

I hate them, briefly.

The atmosphere changes here, melting into foliage and birdsong. This will happen a lot on this route. Oxwich is a

Oxwich Bay

gorgeous mix of shaded woodland, dramatic cliffs and breezy fields, all set above an old village of pastel-coloured cottages and narrow lanes. I'm now in a high woodland, slipping over leaf-mulch and tangled roots as I follow the path. I would recommend doing this run without headphones; there's something truly beautiful about hearing the hiss of waves beside you, only just visible in creases of flint-blue between the trees.

As a Swansea girl, I have never coped well with being locked into cities, away from the sea. Though my swimming skills are poor, something about just knowing it's there, like an old friend, is somewhat soothing.

'You doing okay?' Ian asks, tap-dancing his way over loose stones and roots.

I frown and tell him I'm absolutely fine, but the truth is my mood hasn't yet shifted fully to a more positive place. My jaws are clamped as I bounce sideways down another set of steps (there are lots, but don't worry, they only go downwards this time), realising my shin splints haven't quite healed fully from a few weeks ago.

Running can make you more at peace and appreciative of your body, but it can also cause you to become more frustrated with it. Shin splints are a painfully common affliction in runners – a rite of passage when increasing mileage or having not quite found the perfect shoe. I have been through *so many shoes*. As I bounce down each step, wincing, I can't help but tell myself I'll never be as fast as I once was, or that I'll never be able to do a marathon again.

My last effort was Newport Marathon in 2019, where I was thrilled with a 03:56 marathon time. However, there's still some nagging part of me that wants to do it again, but do it better. I'll always wonder whether I can train hard enough for a 03:30 marathon. When you're a runner, you can end up becoming so fiercely competitive with yourself to the point that you push yourself beyond your limits. When you're fully in it, rest days are mentally tough. Because of this, I didn't run a single race in 2024. Running has become solely an outlet for creativity and better mental health rather than chasing PBs (and self-inflicted injuries). Slowly, through taking this approach, I've become less focused on time. Sometimes I don't upload my runs to Strava. Sometimes I cover my watch. Sometimes I don't measure anything at all and just run until my head feels clear.

But there's always a moment or two that will catch me out; when I see other people's celebratory race photos with their PBs announced and medals flung around their necks, I can't help but feel annoyed with myself. I can't help but think, *what if?*

Trail running, I've discovered, helps to shut off that competitiveness.

Trail running is not like road running. Road running is linear and purposeful; an exercise in efficiency. Trail running, on the other hand, is messy, unpredictable, and wonderfully unhinged. It's a fight against roots that want to trip you, stones that catch beneath your step, and puddles that will win no matter how clever you think your footwork is. It's about relinquishing control and leaning into the chaos of the terrain, however nature intended it to be.

This, I think, is why trail running worms its way into your creativity. Out on the trails, you can't plan every step; you just have to react. Your mind focuses on the immediate: the way the path curves unexpectedly, the texture of the mud underfoot, the low branch that has you ducking awkwardly at the last second. And in doing so, it makes room for the deeper thoughts to surface.

This connection to nature isn't an Instagram filter or a hollow caption about "being one with the earth". It's physical. You feel it in the sting of brambles against your shins, the squelch of mud that invades even the most expensive trail shoes. Out on these trails, nature isn't simply curated for your enjoyment. It's raw, unruly, and indifferent to your ego. And God, this indifference is liberating. Running through a forest or across a ridgeline reminds you that the world is bigger,

older, and more significant than your insecurities about whether that line you've written is working, or if your latest draft is the worst thing you've ever written.
And creativity thrives in that space.
Navigating the slippery trails, you don't think in straight lines, either. Ideas come in fragments, half-sentences that float to the surface alongside the breath you're struggling to catch. A poem begins, not always neatly, but often as a single word that's snagged itself on a low-hanging branch and smacks you in the face. By the time you've tripped over a root and swiped at the mud smeared across your knees, you've caught a line or two in your head. They may not be brilliant yet, but they're there. Write them down.

★

We reach the bottom of the steps and follow the path right, the light sporadically flashing in cadmium green bursts through the trees. I'm in my stride now. I'm aware of the environment around me, absorbing it all.
When you do this run yourself, try and really notice everything.
Listen to the shore. Feel the bitter breeze. Look up briefly at the light. Taste the salt in the air. Smell the earth churning below your feet. Even if you feel like the most useless person in the world at meditation (which you can't be, because that's definitely me), use all five senses and get yourself *present*.

> *Stare hard enough and I'll see*
> *the bright umbrellas of jellyfish wink at the edge,*
> *the kestrel hanging still, nailed in the forest's throat.*

I pause and tap the lines into my phone. Maybe something will grow from them. Maybe it won't. In any case, I'm writing. And that's something that tells me my mind is slowly, ever so stubbornly, opening up creatively to the world around me.

Honestly, don't be a poet. It's an emotional bloody rollercoaster.

*

The forest is dense now. The light around me deepens to a richer green, vines and branches obscuring any sign of where I'm headed next. The path is clear, but slippery as we run upwards, gently, the shoreline hissing beside us out of sight. A squirrel scuttles across the path and disappears to our left where, behind the trees, sheer cliffs plunge into the waves.

We scream at Ted to stop chasing, but he ignores us, his stubborn Jack Russell nature overtaking any sense of immediate danger.

Eventually, he reappears, unfazed and his mouth devoid of small squirrels. That's when we notice, behind him, a break in the trees – a small opening that leads to a scramble of rocks and a long slope that disappears into the sea. By now the clouds are breaking, and the waves are rumpled with ribbons of sunlight.

We clamber down.

This part, of course, is entirely optional to you. But if you want to really experience the mix of landscapes that Oxwich offers, it's worth the little climb down to pause beside the water, mussel shells cracking beneath your running shoes. The breeze is cold and sharp; turn to your left and you'll more often than not see cold-water swimmers and excitable dogs splashing in the freezing tide.

In the eighteenth and nineteenth centuries, the main bay that you are looking towards was frequented by smugglers. They moved upon its tide silently, carrying their dark boats closer, then allowing it to pull them upshore in the dead of night. I imagine their hands: wet, salt-roughened, the shape of them carved from years of lifting, hauling, burying. I imagine them working in silence, their voices pared down to gestures, their lanterns bruising the fog. It's hard to imagine now, in the morning light, but if you stop here on an overcast winter afternoon, you'll find that Gower's darker history is easier to summon.

For all their roguish charm and dangerous allure, the smugglers didn't always win. They might have been smart enough to ferry barrels of contraband under the noses of the authorities and resourceful enough to disappear into the night, but occasionally, they displayed a staggering lack of subtlety. Nowhere is this more evident than in the ill-fated event that unfolded on Oxwich Sands in 1804.

That night, a cutter – a small, nimble boat perfect for a smuggler's activities – dropped anchor in the bay under the cover of darkness. The crew, feeling somewhat cocky, sent two men ashore to ask for directions to Highway Farm, a major staging post for one of Gower's biggest smuggling gangs.

In other words, they rowed across the open water, trudged up the sand, and politely enquired how best to reach their illicit HQ.

The two men they stopped on the beach seemed obliging enough. They provided detailed directions as though they were simply locals eager to point a lost tourist toward the nearest pub.

Satisfied, the smugglers returned to the cutter, and the operation got underway.

By midnight, barrels of contraband (which included brandy, silk, tea, and all the other treasures a Georgian dinner party might need) were being hauled to Highway. The goods were then hidden in secret cellars. It was, for all intents and purposes, a textbook smuggling run.

Until it wasn't.

It turns out that the two helpful fellows on the beach were actually members of the preventive authorities. These were men who'd perfected the art of feigned nonchalance and were probably nudging each other in the ribs and laughing hysterically as they strolled away.

At dawn, the raid began and the customs men descended upon Highway. At first, their searches yielded nothing. The cellars, snug beneath their earthen blanket, remained hidden, but persistence eventually paid off. The chambers were discovered, and with them, 420 barrels of contraband.

The haul was then loaded onto carts, and the convoy began its journey to Swansea. By this time, a crowd of 200 people – farmers, fishermen, and opportunists – gathered along the road, demanding their share of the haul. If I was about then, I probably would have done the same to be honest.

Faced with the possibility of an angry mob and a few pitchforks, the authorities relented, cracking open a few barrels to placate the crowd (who needed Wind Street?). It worked, though 17 of them still mysteriously disappeared before the convoy reached Swansea. Even when the guard on the barrels was increased to 50 men, the commanding officer, knowing full well that no man can resist the offer of free booze, gave his men permission to drink while on duty.

By the time the barrels reached Swansea, the spirits had flowed in every direction; by this, I mean into the villagers' cups, the soldiers' bellies, and into the seas of Oxwich Bay.

It sounded like one hell of a party.

As we sit and watch the waves spilling foam over the rocks, Ted tries to snap at them with his jaws fruitlessly, foam splashing back into his tiny russet-coloured face. His jaws shut, the foam retaliates, and he retreats, bewildered but determined, his tiny face now damp and wrinkled with rage The relentless tide churns on, oblivious to his fury, providing a moody contrast to the gleaming inky crescents of mussel shells nestled in the sand.

I signal to Ian that it's time to climb back up and keep on running.

The forest greets us once more, its dense green canopy gradually loosening its grip to allow the sunlight through in dappled bursts. The air is heavy with the warm promise of autumn, a season that's probably compensating for the biblical deluge of the summer past, one of the wettest summers on record.

Eventually those tangled roots ease off, giving way to a gravelly cliff-path with breathtaking views. This is what it's like to run with nature. On one side, the cliffs rise solid and imposing, their jagged edges softened by the creeping fingers of grass and the wind's persistent hiss. On the other side, the sea sprawls into the horizon, its colour shifting with the light: dull pewter one moment, a streak of silver the next.

My feet fall into a rhythm that feels easier now. My thoughts: those sharp-edged, tangled things that weighed me down at the start, begin to soften. I'm in my stride. Lines aren't just starting in my head, they're finishing, too. Whether they're any good, I can't say, but they're happening, and I let them exist without fighting.

I almost want to spend the rest of the afternoon writing.

*

We push on along the cliffs for a little while, just a woman, a man and a tiny, wild dog. Around us, wildflowers cling stubbornly to the rock, bright shocks of colour against washed-out grey.

Eventually, the path ascends and gives way to a vast field. I soon realise we are not alone.

A herd of them stands scattered across the field, chewing their cud and staring at me with that disinterested judgment that cows are so good at. I've never been comfortable around cows. They're enormous and excellent at staring contests.

Clipping Ted's lead back onto his collar, we slow down to a walk so as not to startle them and keep to the left so we can make the most of the views. Fields of green and gold stretch out towards the sea, some of them freckled with grazing sheep, some gently waving with crops and some lined with the caravans of one of many popular Gower holiday parks.

I should warn you: directions in these parts have a knack for veering from a little ambiguous to downright infuriating. At one point, we find ourselves tracing loops like a pair of slightly bewildered greyhounds, circling the same patch of field in search of the right gate. Should we retrace our steps? Press on? Consult the GPS? Oh, wait, we can't. It doesn't work.

If you have satellite navigation, let it guide you toward Oxwich Castle. If not, enjoy the thrill of deciphering cryptic signposts while savouring the pleasing scratch of grass beneath your trainers after a morning spent hauling yourself uphill.

Whatever you choose to do, don't follow our example of hugging the field's perimeter like really shit ice-skaters.

Go straight and eventually, you'll reach a path that leads past the beautiful Oxwich Castle. Oxwich Castle, for me, is a place steeped in nostalgia. It's one of the first writing residencies I took part in with Literature Wales, *Weird and Wonderful Wales*, back in 2017. Here I got to spend two days wandering the Tudor manor participating in workshops, listening to folk stories and histories based in Gower, then writing responses to it. I was fresh-faced and hopeful.

This was long before I frequently lost my head over deadlines.

This run, I suppose, is a return home to the beginning of my writing journey. We pause outside and hold our phones up to its walls, now verging on honey-coloured in the autumn sunlight.

Oxwich Castle isn't a castle in the storybook sense that we're used to. There are no turrets, no drawbridges and no ghosts that I'm aware of. It's more of a fortified manor, a big statement piece from the sixteenth century designed to say, "Look how important I am", rather than "Please don't invade me". The Mansel family, who built it, were more concerned with showing off their wealth than fending off marauders. Its mock-military flourishes are all about social climbing rather than defence.

In 1541, Sir Rice Mansel began transforming what was once a medieval castle into an impressive Tudor manor. Its intricate windows were designed to let in as much light as possible, and it boasted elegant chimneys and wide stone walls. It was a masterpiece designed to impress the Welsh gentry and make the Mansels look like the Kardashians (or whatever the equivalent was) of sixteenth-century Gower.

However, history is rarely straightforward, is it? By the time Rice's son, Edward Mansel, took over, the family's fortunes were precarious. Edward poured even more money into the place, adding an opulent south wing, complete with fancy rooms and plastered ceilings that wouldn't look out of place on one of my ridiculous home improvement Pinterest boards.

And then things went a bit wrong. The Mansel family's fortunes dwindled, and by the seventeenth century, Oxwich Castle became a money pit. Parts of it were abandoned, left to the elements, the ivy, and the eyes of curious passers-by.

Looking at it now, you can see where time has had its way. The stone walls are weathered, their edges softened by centuries of wind and rain. The windows, once proud frames for light and luxury, blink out over the fields, their glass long gone.

Standing here in my muddy Asics trainers and twenty-first-century sports attire, it's hard not to feel the weight of its history. You can almost see Sir Rice, standing in the courtyard, planning his next addition, or Edward, obsessing over the details of his plasterwork while the family fortunes run dry. You feel for them, weirdly.

It's clear to me now why this would have been such a great choice of location for a writing workshop. And if you're not planning on interrupting your run to explore it today, do come back and spend time here. It's hard not to feel inspired.

Some good news from Ian: we're nearing the end of the run and, of course, the promise of cake. We jog past Oxwich Castle and find that it's downhill all the way to the picturesque village of Oxwich. Its narrow lanes twist and turn, tight enough to keep you alert. The cottages hold their colours lightly: a pale pink that never quite pops into full rose, a blue the colour of storms.

Ted is back on his lead now, still pulling ahead. Ian and I are less physically energetic, though somehow more mentally awake.

Oxwich, I think, wants you to stumble upon its history

instead of screaming it out. It's a place that lets the bay and the cliffs do all the shouting while it leans back, waiting for you to notice what it has to say. And in researching this route, I discovered that this place *does* have a lot to say. I love these quiet, history-filled places. They're where stories are uncovered, layer by beautiful layer.

*

The wooden table beneath my arms feels sturdy and reassuring. I'm tired, hungry and my blood sugars are heading low (as my insulin pump has kindly blared to warn me no less than five times since reaching Oxwich village). Around me, other tables hum with quiet chatter, the air thick with the mingling smells of coffee, seaweed, and someone's vinegar-drenched chips.

As I free the pump from my sports bra to tell it that it's quite okay and that I'm not dead yet, the parasol above just about shields me from the sun that's been unexpectedly generous by late morning. I feel the urge for an ice-cold Coke, rattling with ice. The screen blinks at me: *3.2mmol*. The down arrow tells me I need sugar, fast.

Ian and I decide to share a carrot cake with coffee. It's a generous slab; the top is crowned with a thick layer of cream cheese frosting, wonderfully tangy. A few walnuts cling to the sides, and there's the faintest dusting of cinnamon.

Cake really is an otherworldly experience after a good run. There's something about that mix of exhaustion and sugar that transforms it from a simple baked treat to a small miracle. I do not care how many crumbs I drop down my sports bra.

By the time I scrape the last bit of sugary residue from the plate and chase it down with the final dregs of Americano, I think I'm revived. Maybe even inspired?

Oxwich Bay

A crab wrestles in its shingle pit. I keep sprinting forward, pumping the earth's chest as though I can keep it breathing, my hair whipped in its exhale, pumping its heart with my heel.

Later, I snap my Notes app shut with a sense of satisfaction. Maybe, just maybe, there's a poem buried in today's run, waiting to find its shape.

Running is a little bit magic like that.

Parkmill and Three Cliffs

Location
Parkmill and Three Cliffs, Gower
SS 54360 89230

Distance
Approx. 8K

Parking
The Gower Heritage Centre and Shepherd's.

Facilities
Toilets, food, drink and post-run fuel (i.e. cake) can be found at Shepherd's or The Gower Heritage Centre. For a traditional pub meal and post-run pint, The Gower Inn offers plenty, too.

Tips
Don't leave without popping by the Little Valley Bakery (right next to the Heritage Centre). Their bread and pastries grace some of Swansea's finest cafes for a reason. And anyway, you'll have earned it.

Parkmill and Three Cliffs

It's the 29th December, in that confusing limbo between Christmas and New Year; by this point my diet has consisted mainly of Chocolate Oranges and my body is crying out for both physical exercise and vegetables in any form. This particular morning has made putting off the post-festive run less daunting; the winter air is sharp and clean, like biting into a cold apple. It's nothing short of refreshing after days spent wrapped in a dressing-gown like an overgrown baby, blasted by central heating and the perpetual wink of Christmas lights disturbing my peripheral vision.

You might remember that I mentioned Parkmill earlier, on the drive towards Oxwich. It's the little village that smells succulently of wild garlic during the summer months; in winter, smoke drifts from cottage chimneys in languid ribbons. The trees, once thick, now beat their spiky branches against the December breeze.

It seems like we're not the only people in desperate need of fresh air. The car parks are nearly full, but we manage to squeeze into the last space outside Shepherd's, zipping keys into our pockets before heading towards the charming little stream that runs alongside the Heritage Centre. I feel a little sluggish, but attribute that to the sheer amount of Miniature Heroes I've consumed over the past week.

We begin our run outside the Gower Heritage Centre and its twelfth-century corn mill.

Here's a little bit of its history: the mill contains original equipment from past centuries including millstones imported from France.[3] This mill was part of the sprawling estate of the Le Breos family, who were handed sovereignty over Gower in

1203 (you'll hear their name a lot in Gower history). Farmers weren't tentatively invited to bring their oats and barley here. In fact, they were compelled to, under threat of fines from the estate court.

The Le Breos family were basically the OG drama queens of Gower, constantly embroiled in feuds with rivals like the de Newburg family of Warwick. These feuds were never just about who owned what. To be honest, it was more about staying alive long enough to hold onto it.

The Normans decided to shake things up even more. They booted out the local Welsh inhabitants, shipped in farmers from Somerset and North Devon, and in the process, laid the groundwork for centuries of cross-Bristol Channel connections. This is why some of the words in Gower dialect sound like a quirky, linguistic love-child of Wales and the West Country. The peninsula itself was split into two distinct vibes: the 'Welsherie' in the north, where Welsh was spoken by communities like Penclawdd and Llanrhidian, and the English-speaking areas down south and in places like Llangennith in the northwest. It's no wonder Ian and I take the mick out of each other's differing Welsh accents non-stop. Every time I ask for a 'juice' at a bar and pronounce it *JEH-WSS,* he buckles. (Whatever you say, *JY-OOS*-boy).

Today, fresh flour is still ground in the mill most days – if you've got an hour after your run (and even if you don't, make one), it's worth taking a tour of the centre. Containing a replica cottage, a farming museum, along with a working woodturner's room, woollen mill and blacksmith's, it's a glimpse into the past worth exploring, particularly if history is your thing.

The more I run, the more historically nerdy I find myself becoming. I bloody love boring people with it.

★

I'm with Ian again for this run, partly for the company and partly because he's a born-and-bred South Gower boy whose

Parkmill and Three Cliffs

head is stuffed with facts about any of the routes around here we choose to take. He's not as enthusiastic about the run this time. He's eaten far too much clementine cheesecake.

'Ready to go?' I ask him, knowing full well the answer is no. There's an unspoken, mutual desire to get back in the car and go home to watch *Chicken Run*.

Often, the road to cross the little stream from the water mill is barricaded by a 'diversion' sign as the water rushes down. Not wanting to soak our shoes before we've even started, we cross the small wooden bridge to the road that leads to Park Wood. Interesting fact for fellow Strava geeks: there is a segment of this road that once caused outrage due to the time record being unbeatable, mainly due to the fact someone forgot to turn their run off while they were driving home. Was it cheating? Was it simply a case of an exhausted runner's brain, deprived of carbs? No one knows. No one ever will.

Park Wood, or *Coed y Parc* as it's called in Welsh, appears behind an easily accessible gate on the right and was once a medieval deer park of the Le Breos estate. The run starts gently enough, with a gravel path taking us through an open area of grass, trees and white winter air. I notice an interesting-looking jumble of rocks on the left, and as we move closer, I see that it's essentially a large tomb. This is known as Long Cairn or Giant's Grave, and a sign beside the structure offers more insight:

> *This monument was erected in the neolithic age 3,000 - 1,900 BC for the communal burial of the dead. It was originally covered by a mound of stones and this has been partially restored.*

The remains of 40 humans were discovered here, in a time before individual burials became commonplace. All were adults apart from three.[4] If only I were a writer of Gothic horror.

However, I do at least have a few little writing ideas to take with me today. I always get nostalgic during this part of the year and find myself wanting to write that one final poem before 2024 is done.

Unfortunately, none of them have anything whatsoever to do with large burial chambers.

Although I've come to Park Wood often over the past year to walk Ted, this is the first time I've run it. I know that just a few hundred metres beyond the burial chamber there's a sign to Cathole Cave, a natural feature in the limestone with an entrance over 15 metres high.[5] I leave Ian at the bottom of the hill (he's pausing to attend to some urgent calf stretches) and bounce up the hill hoping the gods of writing will toss forth a thunderbolt of inspiration. You can skip this little cave visit entirely if you want to stick to the path, but while you're here I'd say it's worth a quick look.

Plus, creativity has a habit of finding us when we stray from our usual paths, catching us wonderfully off-guard.

It's a steep but short climb (thankfully). The air is thick with the bitter tang of crushed leaves, the softened rot of life returning to the earth. The fine fronds of light that push through branches cast a coppery glow across my path. About halfway up this hill I find Cathole Cave, protected by a thick metal grille. The stone around it is slick with moisture, as though the sun has never broken this deep through the foliage.

Historians say the cave was once used as a shelter by Mesolithic hunters and as a Neolithic ossuary. It is believed that corpses may have been placed in the caves in this wood until they decomposed, when the bones were moved to the tomb of Long Cairn.

I open the Notes app on my phone and tap out some lines:

> *When you come back, they're lighter.*
> *The weight gone, only the shape left—*
> *a femur, a jawbone, a finger curved*
> *like a misplaced apostrophe.*

This doesn't come to me instantly. In fact, I spend a good five minutes staring into the cave's yawning maw, trying to imagine the bloom of rot, sinew slackened, the white ridge of a human spine protruding from the earth.

I quite like the personification of Stephen King's muse in his wonderful book *On Writing*. If the muse was indeed a person, mine would be folding its newspaper, sighing, taking one long drag of its cigarette then reluctantly tossing me a line or two to work with every now and then, usually at the most inconvenient of times.

I take those lines and I hold onto them as if they're a bag of valuable jewels, because in this strange, messy process of creativity, I guess they are. It doesn't matter if they lead nowhere. It doesn't matter if they end up gathering dust at the back of a notebook, snubbed and unloved. The muse is never consistent and not always easy to work with. It shows up when it feels like it, often late, often reluctant, but nevertheless always so very welcome.

Sometimes, this can go on for months (or even years): waiting for scraps, filling pages with half-sentences, thoughts that don't quite land. I might catch myself wondering if the muse is even still with me or if she's slipped out into the ether to leave me scrambling for ideas. But I always maintain hope that she'll come back (I use 'she' because my muse, in my mind's eye, looks like Cruella de Ville, chain smoking with an arched eyebrow). Every now and then, when I'm focused on nothing but the path I'm running, she'll drift over, flick her cigarette ash into the leaves, and give me something that startles me. It might be a line that crackles. Or an idea that feels alive in my hands. Or perhaps simply something that might just lead somewhere, if I don't choose to fob it off, which happens far too often.

'You alright up there?' Ian is at the bottom of the hill, having worked through every possible stretch in his inventory.

I trample back down, trying not to slip where the mulch has become damp from the previous week's relentless downpours. If you're someone who just likes to get their workouts done and over with, never run with a writer.

★

We're back on the gravel now, an easy, flat run that leads to a crossroads. Ahead of us is the Gower Way, a 56km path mapped out to mark the Millennium by The Gower Society.

Today, we're turning left because we bloody love a hill and also because we do not want to run 56km after a week of charcuterie boards and prosecco.

As far as hills go (about a mile in this case), this one isn't the worst. It's a gradual incline, with a few twists and turns along the way. We're still on a gravel path, so there's no risk of slipping and falling on my backside which is always a plus. There's nothing around us here but the quiet hiss of wind in the trees, the rhythm of our trainers hitting the ground and the unmistakable sound of two runners pretending they're not out of breath.

Things even out once we get to a bend in the track. We stop for a moment, pretending to admire our surroundings. The trees here are utterly bare, forked against the grey sky, their branches sketched out like someone had flicked them into being with charcoal. Neither of us says anything about the real reason we've stopped. It's an unspoken pact between runners: sometimes, you just need a moment. It's no big deal. Sometimes, it's a relief if your partner stops when you're trying to hold back from admitting you'd like to pause too.

The incline continues, gradually, until it finally crests onto a long, forgiving track that drops down towards the road at Penmaen.

We stop again, not because we're tired though. There's no pretending we're just adjusting a shoelace or checking our phones. It's the view.

From above the church of St John the Baptist in Penmaen, there's a little patch of grass that gives you the most breathtaking view of Three Cliffs Bay. You'll recognise these iconic three cliffs from the labels on anything Gower-based, whether that's the "ales of natural beauty" from Gower Brewery, necklaces from Pa-Pa Jewellery in Parkmill or even at gigs (e.g. a gig for The Amazons concert in Cardiff. The Gower-themed art thrilled me no end).

Here, in person, it's a different thing altogether. The cliffs rise, dark and jagged, while the bay stretches out below, its waters shifting between greys and blues.

Once we've pulled enough poses with the dramatic cliffs in the background, we follow the path down past the church and reach the road we need to cross in Penmaen. There's a sign for Three Cliffs Holiday Park which takes us down a little path. When doing this route yourself, you'll know it's the right one because there's a little mirror mounted on the corner – allegedly it's for road safety, but it doubles nicely as a wind-blown selfie check.

I take photos a lot when running. Not necessarily of myself, but of the landscapes. I particularly love taking photos of the scenes I see every day; since starting running in 2005 along Loughor Estuary, I've taken so many photos of that route. And every single day, it reveals itself differently. Different light. Different seasons. Different weather. Different time of day. I could line up all those photos of the same place over the years and you'll rarely see two the same, and there's something beautiful about that. Every day, and every run, is a brand new start.

The road down to Three Cliffs Holiday Park is a narrow, hedge-lined ribbon of asphalt that curves unremarkably through the landscape. I mean, it's functional, but it's not the most inspiring section of the run; there's little to photograph here unless you're curating an album titled *The Gates and Hedges of Gower*. But running isn't always about striking scenery. Sometimes it's more about those little moments along the way that inspire you.

Like, for example, the family in their brightly coloured

Dryrobes, striding cheerfully with two springer spaniels in tow. They beam at us as we pass, shouting a hello with a gusto that definitely gives them away as being in holiday mode. We pass a driver of an Audi who, in an act of rare courtesy, actually waves after we've flattened ourselves against the hedgerow to let her inch by.

Beyond that, it's more hedges, gated fields, and a low hum of conversation; mostly Ian filling me in on the Gower gossip like he's the region's unofficial historian. Basically it's about who's sold what, who's in the middle of some fence-based feud, and who's turned their barn into a boutique yoga retreat. It's oddly fascinating and weirdly hyper-specific. I love this stuff.

Eventually, the holiday park appears, but we're not stopping. Just before the park, the path veers right, a subtle turn that takes us out of the suffocating narrow hedgerows and into a less tamed landscape. Like a curtain lifting, the views slowly reveal themselves; Notthill's path teases us with an increasingly spectacular panorama of cliffs, sea, and sky. I can almost see the ridges in those three iconic cliffs and almost pick out the brave swimmers pushing through the water's freezing swell. Bonkers.

When I first started running, at the tender age of sixteen, I never imagined that it would be something that would become so incorporated in my life; that I'd feel the *itch* to go and push myself for miles after days of Christmas overindulgence. Before, I would have had to talk myself into it. When I first started, I spent 50% of those initial 20-minute jogs crying in a hedge, convinced I was going to die of calf cramp and a lack of oxygen.

But then I experienced my first-ever post-run high. As I'd soap myself in the shower, face still apple-red, the ache felt oddly ... *nice*. I'd done something. No, I'd *defied* something. Something like that little critical voice in my head that told me I was too unfit and uncool to do anything sporty. Something like the PE teachers who rolled their eyes when I once again missed a serve in rounders and went to hide behind the changing block. Something like the kids at school who laughed at every single thing I did because to them I was a walking joke.

Maybe running isn't cool. Writing definitely wasn't cool as a kid. Maybe it still isn't that cool. Either way, at thirty-four, I don't care. I'm not here to fit in.

My first motivation to run was to lose weight so that the bullies wouldn't comment on my body anymore. Of course, hindsight reveals the ridiculousness of it all: there was nothing wrong with me. They'd have picked on my haircut instead (fringe ridiculously swept over the eye, completely obscuring my vision on my left side), or my shoes, or the way my voice shook even if it was only to answer the register. But at the time, I believed them. And so I ran, praying I'd somehow shrink out of sight.

At first, it was agony. Running is honestly not fun when you've just started. Your chest burns like you've been eating lit cigarettes and your legs feel like sacks of wet cement. Worst of all, you're completely exposed. There's no hiding when you run. You're just out there, flailing and puffing, hoping nobody you know drives past. I wasn't even dressed for running, not really – unless cargo pants and a Green Day t-shirt is the next look for Team GB. Then came the 'runner's high': a phrase so overused you stop believing it until you feel it for yourself. I know it's real because I became one of those people. You know the ones: cornering acquaintances at parties to evangelise about race routes and endorphins while ignoring their eyes glazing over (to all the victims I've bored at staff parties about my running routes: I owe you a mojito).

The more I ran, the less it became about the bullies. It became about me, and how running was a tiny respite in a world that had become a bit too loud and cruel. It became my escape. Of course, the bullies found out about it eventually. They always do. And they added it to their list of grievances against me. "Oh, she runs now? What a freak." They'd then pantomime what a whale looks like while running.

I mean, whales can't even run.

But when I was out on the muddy trail to the estuary, I didn't care. I felt free. Ask any runner and they'll wax lyrical about the clarity that comes mid-stride, and the way problems untangle themselves along the way. Studies back it up, though they're hardly needed by those who've felt it firsthand. A 12-week running program, for instance, for adults and children with clinical diagnoses of various mood disorders resulted in significant reductions in anxiety, stress, and depression.[6] I can vouch for the improvements in mood; I'm very often a different person entirely post-run, particularly if I've left my desk, grumbling, to clear my mind on a lunchtime 10K.

Somewhere along the way, I stopped running from myself. I stopped being the shy girl who ducked out of PE lessons or wielded the excuse of a mysteriously endless menstrual cycle (always conveniently on a Monday afternoon) to avoid swimming. Instead, I became someone who wrote stories in her head while pounding down country lanes. I became someone who felt alive with the thrill of movement. Someone who let her mind and body run wild.

And perhaps, most importantly, someone who finally felt just that tiny bit more comfortable in her own skin.

This same high is with me right now as I try to keep my balance after Ian, pummelling down the dusty path to the sand. At the bottom, I can't help but leap onto the stones at Pennard Pill, even though we have no intention of plunging into the sea today. I'm not alone in this tiny joy – there's a procession of adults, children, and dogs, all hopping over the smooth stepping stones, arms pinwheeling, trying not to tumble into the shallow water.

We continue onwards, leaving the stones to shrink from view behind us. In the damp winter seasons, you've got two options here:

1) Stay on the left-hand side and battle your way ankle-deep in mud before reaching the woods.

2) Stay on the right-hand side and push through the sand until you reach the woods a little earlier.

Having tried both (for research purposes, obviously), I recommend the second option, mainly because it's really uncomfortable trying to enjoy a post-run coffee when your socks are squelching inside your shoes. Unless, of course, mud is your thing, in which case I hope it thrills you much as you want it to.

My legs are getting a little sore as we push up through the sand, the river twisting beside us and Pennard Castle grand against the sky on our right-hand side. Sometimes, you may find cows grazing beside the river, heaving their huge bodies and tearing up clods of grass. Not today.

Thank God.

A path appears to the right and we follow it through the trees, the sand giving way to damp earth and tangled roots. Apart from a few walkers in the distance, there's nothing much to look at now but the thick wall of trees and a stream hissing on our left.

From here, it's easy. The path takes us back towards Parkmill, the sound of cars rumbling back into earshot. Then there's a right turn and we reach a tiny wooden bridge, slumped charmingly between the trees. My stomach is grumbling; I've been over an hour without a segment of Terry's Chocolate Orange.

We cross the road and return to the Gower Heritage Centre, ready to warm up with coffee. In summer, the tables outside heave with cider festival goers, a sunburned crowd of swaying humans happily numbing themselves to the fact that they'll have to stand up again eventually. In January, the village welcomes Mari Lwyd: a slightly terrifying horse skull on a stick, festooned with ribbons and steeped in Welsh tradition.

Today, outside, it's quiet. Inside, we're presented with fresh pastries, cakes, Welsh chocolates, coffee, books on Gower and (joy of joys!), free Welsh cake samples. Today, it's a very seasonable cranberry. The cranberries peek out like tiny rubies, swaddled by buttery, crumbly dough. I take one, thanking the server a bit too eagerly, my mind already drafting my apology for the second one I know I'm going to take. The great thing about running is that my blood sugars always head low after an hour, which means a sweet treat isn't just a reward. It's medicinal! My insulin pump isn't beeping yet, but it's only a matter of minutes before it warns me of an oncoming hypo.

We take two coffees and an apple and blackberry flapjack outside to share. A pair of walkers wrestle their map in the breeze, its corners flapping, while a group of children shriek with joy at absolutely nothing. Everyone seems to have somewhere to go, but no one is in much of a hurry to get there. There's a runner, too, gliding by effortlessly, their face serene. Watching them, I feel that familiar itch, a voice in my head that always kicks in at times like this: *You could just go and do it all again.*

Running always finds a way to get under your skin. It leaves you sitting there, crumbs in your lap, half-listening to other people's lives, and already planning the next slog through the mud. The espresso is gone in three sips, the flapjack reduced to sticky smears on my fingertips, and still, I find myself glancing at the path ahead, wondering where's next.

Castell Coch

Location
Castell Coch, Tongwynlais, near Cardiff
ST 13202 82656

Distance
Approx. 5K

Parking
Castell Coch car park – small, so get there early to avoid circling like a vulture in Lycra. Alternatively, there's plenty of parking on the road outside.

Facilities
Toilets, cafe, picnic area, and a very whimsical castle.

Tips
Stop and have a peek in the castle if you can before your run. It's magical enough outside, but inside it's a visual and historical feast.

Castell Coch

Today's run is a short one, but what it lacks in distance it makes up for in elevation at the starting line (sorry, hill-haters). The date on my car dashboard tells me it's January 25th: St Dwynwen's Day. I have nothing romantic planned; I simply told Ian I was off for a run and ended up somehow getting pulled towards this location, enchanted by its fairytale appearance, after seeing it pop up on trail recommendations.

Driving up the motorway, I tried to drown out my thoughts with acoustic folk music. You know, the sort you tend to mostly hear in adverts for fancy oat milks or expensive coffee. But my brain wasn't having it. The playlist barely registered in the clamour that was vying for attention in my head: work deadlines, the looming shadow of tax returns, and that weird January restlessness that sits in my chest like a wet blanket.

When it emerges from the hillside, Castell Coch gives me a little flutter of childlike excitement before I've even parked outside the gates. The car park is closed today. I find a space further down the lane and perform a haphazard manoeuvre. God, I hope I don't get towed. As I step out into the cold, the castle rises above me, all towers and turrets, the sort of place a Disney princess might live if she were on the lookout for handsome Welsh princes.

When I enter the gates, I'm met with a long, steep hill towards the castle and the start of my running route. I'm half-tempted to run it, but then remember that I've never done this trail before and there might well be far more challenging hills in store for me. As I trudge upward, I scroll through playlists, trying to settle on something that might distract me from my laboured breathing later on. Post-rock feels like the right choice: slow builds and soaring crescendos. I'm running alone today, and without music, I'd be left with nothing but the sound of my own wheezing and the wet slap of my trainers against the trail.

There's a group of young lads behind me, puffing once we reach the halfway point, blowing puffs of watermelon ice-flavoured vape into the sky.

"Need to get back in the gym, boys," one of them wheezes. I haven't even *started* yet.

Once I approach the castle, I pause. There's something about its plump turrets and the beautiful woodland art painted on its right-hand side that has me joining the small groups of people all having the same idea and tilting their phones towards it, capturing the beautiful structure in the late afternoon light. Today, the castle is closed. A very detailed display board informs me there is weatherproofing work being done on the roofs and chimneys, as well as extensive re-pointing of stone walls – but if it is open when you come here, please do go and explore inside.

Castell Coch is a nineteenth-century Gothic Revival castle, but while its current incarnation is very much a nineteenth-century daydream brought to life, its roots go much deeper. After 1081, the Normans swept into South Wales, conquered Cardiff, and immediately set about building castles to mark their territory. The first castle at the site was a classic motte-and-bailey affair, its main job to control the Taff Gorge and remind the locals who was in charge. But it was abandoned not long after, possibly because it was about as structurally sound as a damp custard cream.

Fast-forward to the late thirteenth century, and along comes Gilbert de Clare. Unfortunately for Gilbert, the native Welsh rebellion of 1314 had other ideas, and his castle was destroyed. And so, the site slipped back into ruin again. For centuries, it was little more than a pile of mossy rubble tucked away in the woods. But in 1760, Castell Coch entered a new chapter. John Stuart, Third Earl of Bute, acquired the ruins as part of a deal that brought his family vast estates in South Wales.[7]

Enter William Burges. Unlike Bute, Burges didn't have a fortune, but he wasn't doing too badly either, thanks to his dad's success as a civil engineer. More importantly, he had flair – flamboyant, larger-than-life flair, with an imagination that made him the architectural equivalent of Lady Gaga. When the two men met in 1865, it was a bit like opposites attracting. Bute was introverted and Burges was sociable, but they bonded over a shared obsession with all things medieval.

Within a year, Burges had pitched a plan to revamp Cardiff Castle, complete with a tower and an excavated moat garden. For Burges, this was the holy grail of commissions, with an unlimited budget and a blank canvas. In 1871, he turned his attention to Castell Coch. Work began, and Burges went all in. He raised the towers, topped them with conical roofs like something out of a children's storybook, and added copper-gilt weathervanes that twinkled in the sunlight. Inside, he created a medieval fantasy on steroids, complete with timber walkways, central heating (yes, really), and a bell-pull system for visitors to summon servants. Burges's imagination was in overdrive, and Bute loved it.

But then, in 1881, Burges died suddenly, leaving his masterpiece unfinished. His team carried on the work, but things started to change. Gone were the strict Gothic Revival vibes, replaced by softer, more sensual designs inspired by the new Aesthetic Movement. Nature crept into the decor, and the ceilings bloomed with woodland murals, complete with monkeys swinging about. Apparently, the marquis wasn't thrilled about the monkeys, dismissing them as a bit too "lascivious" for his wife's bedroom.

Today, Castell Coch is a natural treasure for newlyweds, film stars, and little people like me, standing here dressed up in running shoes and silly leggings, gawping up in awe.

It's a little bit of joy in this very long month.

★

The start is easy to find; it's waiting for me to the right of the castle, with a map very clearly displayed on a board. Now as you know, I'm no good at reading maps, but even for someone who can't navigate my local Tesco, this one's simple to follow. Paths are marked clearly:

- Sir Henry's Trail – Red
- Burges' Way – Yellow
- Sculpture Discovery Trail – Blue
- Three Bears Cave Walk – Brown

Today, I focus just on Sir Henry's Trail and Burges' Way to bring me nicely up to a 5K. I should point out that there *are* indeed longer routes around Fforest Fawr, which sprawls way beyond the grounds of Castell Coch, but today I want to show you the most popular routes; the ones people come here on a Saturday afternoon especially for. It's one of those trails that's great if you're just starting on trails or if you want to bring your newbie running friend along to join you without them swearing off running forever.

I click my music on, set my watch, and go. I immediately find myself tackling a steep hill. This goes up farther (and more vertically) than I expect it to. There's nothing like an immediate hill to get me wondering if I have, in fact, become desperately unfit overnight, or if it's just the effort of hauling myself uphill above the spiky winter trees. I stop for a second and turn to see how far down below me the castle's turrets have moved. From here, I can see the deep blues and greens of its woodland mural, juxtaposed against the fierce winter light over Tongwynlais. In the distance, a ribbon of blue water unspools itself down the valley, dipping out of my eyeline.

It's a dusty, rocky climb to the top, where I'm met with another map with some facts about each route. As much as I'm intrigued by the caves (and am charmed by the 'Three Bears' name), I can feel my inner child secretly wanting to spot some animal sculptures more than any other landmark.

Things flatten out now, the earth giving way to gravel. It's busy today, and I wish I'd arrived earlier rather than rocking up at 2pm on the sunniest Saturday of the year so far, expecting the unlikely event of uninhabited paths. But, if you're going to do trail running in a place of natural beauty, you have to expect people. Just have the foresight to set an alarm and do it before everyone else is even out of their pyjamas – this also gives you an excellent opportunity to spot a sunrise. Hey, maybe you'll have a brief stint of Instagram virality between breakfast and lunch.

I'll be honest here – because I think it's important I remain honest – I was trying to mentally construct this chapter in my head from the get-go. I've quickly learned that to try and deliberately seek out something to awe and impress at every turn quickly leads to disappointment, frustration, and feelings of failure. Not everyone is here to run today. In fact, I may be the only idiot in running gear. As I bounce lightly up the gravel, overtaking families in their woolly hats and winter coats, I find myself getting infuriated rather than soothed by nature's steady presence. Why couldn't the trees be more unusual? Why is there no showstopping monument, steeped in some ancient lore? Why isn't there something that could get me excitedly researching it the minute I got home?

The castle is grand, sure. But over time, I've learned that my running routes, much like my creative ideas, need space to just *be*. It's not the job of the beeches or sycamores to render me speechless. That's ego talking, its persistent voice whining in my head: "Who can I impress? And *how*? I need to write something remarkable! Eventful!"

I'm aware of it when I'm snapping pictures or tapping out captions to accompany my runs. I want the routes to say something about me; for the audience to think: "Wow, what an amazing trail!" Or for my Strava times to proclaim, "What an amazing time; she's a super-fast runner!"

The fact is: I'm not. Not even close. And that's been more difficult to accept than I'd like to admit at times. We're living in an age where everything, whether we like it or not, has an audience – even if we never choose to share. As a writer, it's the imagined reader peering over my shoulder as I type. As a runner, it's either the person accompanying me or my very modest Strava following, who I imagine must be nudging each other over their post-run protein shake, saying, "Ooh, she's not so fast these days, is she? Shame, she was flying through these routes ten years ago". It's ridiculous, of course. All of it. So why can't I let it go and enjoy the running for what it is?

It's a process of unlearning, that's why. And throughout these chapters, I'll be learning and unlearning a lot.

★

The path tips gently down, the thick forest hedging me in from both sides. There's a slowness to this I want to embrace. No one is moving with much urgency, which at first frustrates me but eventually, I simply give in to it. Between the bare bones of birches, children hurtle over the rust-coloured leaves that have been layering the forest floor since summer's end. Dogs propel themselves after them, snapping at leaves, sniffing at each other and parading sticks between their slobbery jaws. I must bring Ted here next time.

As the path rises gently again, I notice a great wooden bear towering on my left, paws held high as though trying to peer over the trees and down at the castle. Behind it, there's a fenced-off landmark, which I assume means it is important.

And it is. Here we have the Three Bears' Cave, which isn't actually a cave but a series of small, medium and larger holes that are actually the entrance to old iron mines.[8] If you look closely enough, you'll notice that the larger hole is still covered in fake fool's gold, which is a throwback to when it featured in the 1989 BBC TV series *Prince Caspian and The Voyage of the Dawn Treader* (I'm saying this like I've seen it. I haven't). The BBC are pretty fond of this landmark as it goes, so you may also well recognise it from the series *Merlin*, *Sherlock*, *Dr Who*, and *Casualty* too.

There is no filming here today, which is good, because we don't need a wild-haired runner blowing her nose in the background of a good BBC drama.

I continue on my way, following the red signs for Sir Henry's Trail. The woods stretch around me, sparse in their winter dress, but you can tell they're just waiting patiently for spring. Come back when it arrives and the ground will erupt in bluebells and wild garlic, the air thick with sweetness. Come back in autumn (because poets bloody love autumn) and the trees will unlatch their gold leaves, scattering it in great, drifting handfuls: a final, glorious flourish before the long retreat of winter.

To my right, a group of boys are stacking sticks against a tree, building something ramshackle and wonderful: a den, possibly, like something Eeyore would take shelter in. Their faces are pink with cold, fierce with concentration, lost entirely in the act of making. I often see that look in children when I'm taking them through the process of writing stories, too. That thrill of creating something that's all theirs, before their inner critic develops and tries to wrestle it all back.

Nature is often a wonderful reminder of how joyful it is to create something, let it take root, blossom, then start again.

The trail curves round through the forest, the gravel giving way to the mulch of leaves and ghostly birches. This is always the most joyful part of trails – leaving the easy, solid path and letting the terrain carry you where it will. I glance down, just in time to register the mistake in my choices. Road shoes. Thin-soled, no grip, utterly useless on this treacherous mix of wet leaves and deep, sticky mud. These are the sort of shoes that make real trail runners nod solemnly and mutter, "Well, that was a mistake, eh?"

Every step is now a gamble. My weight shifts too far forward, and I catch myself at the last second. A patch of damp mulch slides underfoot, and my arms flail in that cartoonish way, and I realise the run is now in charge of me, not the other way around. And while it's not relaxing in a spa day sort of sense, letting go of control does bring a sort of relief. There's no time to think about what I can concoct from what remains in the fridge for dinner in those annoying two days before the weekly food shop. I'm not thinking about work, or deadlines, or anything else for that matter except trying not to get my ankles hooked on roots or slide onto my arse through the mud. I'm entirely, utterly present.

I follow the signs up until the hill crests and descends towards a little wooden bridge.

It is serene here. No traffic noise, no hum of busy motorways (despite its relatively close proximity to the A470), just the sounds of a place that has been living here long before I decided to clatter through it in stupid footwear. The breeze moves through the undergrowth, rustling the brambles with a soft hush, almost reminiscent of a coastal run. A thrush trills from somewhere in the canopy, its warble high and clear. Beneath me, the stream purrs gently as it threads its way under the bridge, smoothing over pebbles.

I stop. Take a breath. Snap a photo, because that's what we do now – collect tiny, flat versions of moments for likes, instead of just letting them happen. I'll inevitably put up some seemingly profound but ultimately cringey caption to go with it on my Instagram later.

And then I keep moving.

The path straightens out before abruptly turning into something that looks less like a trail and more like the aftermath of a minor geological disaster. The ground collapses into a mess of loose rock, half-formed steps, and the occasional tree root lying in wait for a distracted runner in inappropriate shoes. Below me, walkers are playing an unspoken game of 'The Floor is Lava', wobbling from one dry rock to the next, arms out for balance, faces set in determination. A polite couple, seeing me pummel down the path, let me go ahead. They've been stuck here for longer than they planned.

To my left, the woods plunge into a valley thick with trees and brambles, the green stretching endlessly downwards. It's beautiful and wild, almost inviting me to just pause and reflect.

Like reflecting, for example, on why I chose to wear these bloody road shoes. The soles, smooth and unhelpful, do sod all as I pick my way down, navigating each step like I'm trying to tap-dance over an ice rink. But this is the price of trail running, I guess. These routes are rarely paved for your convenience.

Ahead of me, I recognise the view. It's the road I first started out on. I fly down it, wind whistling past me, my cheeks pinched with cold. I check my watch. I've not even done 3K.

I tell myself I'll run up the hill to the castle this time. I want to do it all again, but with the yellow Burges' Way signs next.

★

After looping the shorter Burges' Way path (which is the same direction, the same horrible vertical climb, but cuts across and involves jumping over fallen trees), I click my watch off at 5K and have nothing left in me to run up the hill to the castle. I'm hoping for coffee, or at least to flop over onto a picnic bench with a bottle of water. The afternoon light is low now, bathing the castle in a coppery glow that only enhances its dreamlike appearance. Settling onto a bench, I gulp down mouthfuls of cold water and flex my fingers inside my gloves.

I'm cold, I'm tired, but after a long winter and a good run, I can feel that brighter days aren't too far away at all.

Caerphilly Mountain

Location
Caerphilly Mountain
ST 15592 85227

Distance
Approx. 11K

Parking
Free parking at Caerphilly Mountain Snack Bar.

Facilities
Toilets, food and drinks at the snack bar.

Tips
Tiptoe very 'caerphilly' over the mud (sorry). Also, either pack a spare pair of shoes or something to wipe the mud off if you don't want your car to look like it's been towed from Shrek's swamp once you get back into it.

Caerphilly Mountain

Caerphilly Mountain, just from the name, sounds like a place that's going to make my legs stronger, which I think is a good thing. I'm not running alone today; I pick up my fellow running friend Inês from Swansea on the way, and there's something to be said about having someone you're accountable to for getting you out of bed early for a mountain run on a Sunday morning. Running alone means you can argue with yourself and perhaps take the scenic route to a café instead. Running with a friend means you actually have to follow through with what you've promised to do, with no excuses.

Inês, like me, is a creative. A visual artist by trade, but also someone who dabbles in poetry. She's the sort of woman you can have proper, soul-enriching conversations with for hours if your Spotify is too embarrassing to put on in the car (no, I don't know how Atomic Kitten ended up on there, thank you). She's the kind of person who will talk about art and books and the vast terrifying beauty of the world without making you feel like an unbearable arse for doing so. I don't often bring these things up with casual acquaintances in the pub, mostly because I am, in my natural state, socially awkward. A weird poet.

As we drive towards Caerphilly, we pass the time cruising the relatively quiet M4 discussing what it is about running trails that keeps us going out there time after time, saturating ourselves in mud.

'It reminds me that I'm lucky,' she says. 'To live here, so close to so many beautiful places that we take for granted. It reminds me why I chose this place.'

I can't help but agree. Until I got into trail running, I hadn't seen quite as many gems tucked into places that are so overlooked or taken for granted. Oxwich and Parkmill, which I had previously only visited infrequently, were now staples on my runs and walks. Brombil Reservoir had completely transformed the dismissive attitude that is so often bestowed upon Port Talbot, with its plumes of factory smoke and industrial landscape. Today, I hope that my first visit to Caerphilly will be one that I associate only with unpredictable trails and untamed nature.

Something wildly, beautifully Welsh.

*

Parking, to my relief, is easy. There are no pay-to-park machines or long queues, which is always a plus. I get out of the car and check my pockets for my glucose supplies. I quickly check my insulin pump; my blood sugars are a little higher than I'd like for a sedentary day, but perfect for a fairly hard trail run.

For navigation, I rely on the AllTrails app, which I thoroughly recommend if, like me, you find that maps just look like an elaborate attempt at abstract expressionism or a bowl of tangled spaghetti.

And yet, despite having this literal GPS-powered idiot-proofing system in my pocket, I immediately go the wrong way. The app, in a tone that I can only describe as passive-aggressive, buzzes at me: "Did you take a wrong turn?"

Why, yes, AllTrails. Yes, I did.

Not only have I missed my starting point, I have, in a spectacular display of misguided enthusiasm, run straight past it and powered my way to the top of the hill, where I now stand, wheezing, admiring a panoramic view that I was absolutely not supposed to see yet. There are two options here. I could pretend this was deliberate, like a pre-run warm-up. I could act like this is a moment of serious reflection before the actual run begins.

Or, I could admit defeat, jog back down, and actually follow the correct trail like I was supposed to if I could read a map. I choose the latter. I'm not a total dick.

*

Downhill is easy. Blissfully easy. I have to call over to Inês a couple of times to pause so I can wrangle my running tights back up over my bum. They're falling down and I realise I've worn the wrong ones: these are the ones I get deadlift PBs in, not the ones I run down mountains in.

The map then takes us across the road and has us dodging cars, which feels bizarre. I'm feeling less at one with nature as a Honda Civic growls past, headed to a pub car park. The pub, as revealed by the large sign standing proudly outside the car park, is called *The Black Cock Inn*.

A little path with a step stile (I know the name of this now because I'm really boring and have researched countryside stiles) takes us over into muddy farmland. And when I say muddy, I mean *muddy*. Thick, glutinous, soul-swallowing mud, pretty much steadfast in its determination to wrestle the shoes clean off your feet. One minute I'm running, half-distracted by the beauty of the brambles tangled with frost and the next, I'm ankle-deep in something that could pass for chocolate cake batter. Each footfall sounds like it's being swallowed.

Both Inês and I are more than a little worried this is the last time we will ever see our shoes. And mine are *brand new*.

I pause, briefly, to snap a photo of the carnage: my right foot, propped on a stile, encased in what looks more like the foot of a bog monster than a running shoe. I text it to Ian: *Can you put running shoes in the washing machine or is that a bad idea?* x

When I was a kid, mud was magic. It meant I'd been adventuring. It meant I'd been busy living. Somewhere between childhood and adulthood, we get obsessed with cleanliness; not just in our bodies, but in our narratives. Everything has to be filtered, polished, or purposeful. But in the middle of a soggy Welsh field, I realise that some of the best bits of life are mucky, messy, and completely pointless. They make you laugh or cry, but at the very least *feel* something. Writers *love* feeling something.

And maybe that's creativity too: the wonderfully unglamorous slog through uncertain terrain. You don't always know where you're going. You slip, lose your footing, lose your enthusiasm then find it again. When you stand back up, you're more full of your story than you were before. This, always, is a good thing.

★

Eventually, we emerge from one more field (after having scrambled over a barbed wire fence, thanks to my inability to listen properly to even a live trail map) to see a drop in front of us – the thrilling sort of drop that as a kid, would make me lie on my side and roll all the way to the bottom.

I resist the temptation and opt, very sadly, to be an adult.

We run. The momentum builds, sending our feet turning over faster and faster as we descend. This, I am convinced, is the moment I slip backwards and take out every dandelion just trying to have a peaceful Sunday.

But I don't. I reach the bottom, a hero. As does my running companion (who I never doubted anyway; she's a seasoned hiker and used to both challenging terrain and climbing walls). The path takes us left and into the woodland.

I realise I've never seen Inês tired on any run or hike we've been on. She pushes forward with a calm composure that I can't help but both envy and admire. It makes me think of how some people chase goals with fierce energy, and others with steady breath. Inês is, impressively, the latter.

★

'That's weird,' says Inês as we follow the track through the woodland. 'The trees. There are branches only on one side, and they're all leaning the same way.'

I turn my head right to look. She's right. She's far more observant than I am; I'm just trying not to fall over.

I stop, breath misting in the cold air, and look properly this time. She's right. The trees aren't just leaning, but kind of look like they're surrendering. Each one is bent like it's mid-bow, branches only growing in one direction, like they've all agreed, telepathically, which way is safest to grow.

Later, I look it up: they're called *flag trees*.

These are trees that have been shaped, year after year, by relentless winds – so much so that they give up trying to fight in all directions. The wind dictates their architecture. The branches on the windward side are starved, snapped, or stripped away, until only one side continues growing. I suppose it's a kind of botanical resilience. Another cause of flag trees is 'winter desiccation': a brutal seasonal culling where the relentless dryness of winter air strips the upwind side of a tree, killing off any chance of growth. Meanwhile, the downwind side continues sprouting limbs as if nothing has happened. Arborists call them flag trees because they resemble flags flapping in the wind, though really, they look more like a woman in a thin coat, walking headfirst into a storm.

I think about how writing ideas find their shape, often just as unexpectedly. What you think you're working on at the start may look nothing like the work you have by the end. We all start with a rough blueprint. But life (and by life I mean wind, and grief, and deadlines, and rejection letters, and those days where nothing you write feels right) starts shaping us. It wears down the parts that once reached out in every direction. We lose pieces of ourselves to the elements. And slowly, we start growing in a particular way, in a particular voice, shaped by what survived.

Some people talk about finding your artistic style like it's this triumphant, pure moment of epiphany, but what if it's more like becoming a flag tree? What if your voice isn't just what you choose, but what remains after everything else got weathered?

> The wind writes them slant,
> presses cold into their backs,
> steering, pushing. They give in,
> or they don't, but either way
> one side stops speaking.

I stop and tap a couple of lines into my phone. Like I've said before, if you want to get your route done and over with, don't run with a writer.

*

We've reached an awkward gate that leads onto a golf course. It takes two of us to wrestle it open, before we work out that we need to lift the metal bar with our feet to move it free. A sign warns us of the risk of getting smacked on the skull with a golf ball which, to be honest, is not how I plan on leaving this world. I didn't come all this way to only reach the halfway point in my run, only to be knocked clean off this earth by a Titleist Pro V1.

Fun fact about Caerphilly Golf Club: its eminent history includes an incident during World War 1 when a member landed his plane on the first fairway.[9] Fortunately, this was a one-off occurrence, and there are no planes to run us over today.

It's a relatively short stretch over the golf course before we're back onto the road and then squelching through mud and grass again. We approach what looks like a quarry to our right, as wild and Welsh as I'd hoped from this run. The walls rise up in slices of earth, the colour of bruised plum, where years of digging have left the land peeled open, raw and exposed. Inês steps forward, carefully picking her way across loose rock, drawn in by the strangeness of the landsccape

I hang back slightly. There's a feeling here, which isn't threatening I don't think, but more like you've walked into someone else's memory and shouldn't touch anything.

Once, hands worked this place. I can picture it if I try hard enough: men with dust-caked brows and calloused palms, splitting stone from stone, dragging the mountain down one piece at a time. Their voices are long gone now, but I can trick myself into believing they might still be caught somewhere, echoing in the crevices, whispering through the moss and shale.

'Is it coal?' I ask. I am wrong. This is Cefn Onn Slate Quarry, the first of two quarries on this run.

The next comes after: Wern Ddu Clay Pit, also known as Coed y Werin, a Geological Site of Special Scientific Interest with 300-million-year-old Carboniferous rocks and coal seams.[10] It's a place where history pushes through the soil discreetly, just to remind us that it's still there.

★

The views open up alongside us as we run on: miles of patchwork fields, sheep grazing in the distance, the slate-coloured clouds slung low. We're on farmland now, running straight towards a muscular bull, shunting his body along the gate to tend to an itch.

'He's friendly!' yells a farmer from the other side of the gate. His accent is thick, Cardiffian. 'He'll try and follow you out of the gate, though. He finishes his food then goes for the food in this field, the greedy bugger.'

Sure enough, as we squeeze ourselves through the smallest possible gap we can make in the wooden gate, the bull presses close; so close I can feel the hot huff of its breath as it treads behind me. As wary as I am about cattle, something about this jovial farmer reassures me. I almost turn back to pat the bull like a puppy, but seeing its colossal size and its proximity to me and the gate, I decide against it.

The gate clatters behind us.

'Have a lovely day!' calls the farmer. We wish him a good day in return, waving as we run downhill.

It's here that I realise I'm tired. Not just a bit sleepy or achey. No, this is the deep, cellular-level exhaustion. I've had a cold all week, and my body is making sure I don't forget it. What should have been a bracing, lung-cleansing run now feels like an ultimate physical challenge, my legs moving beneath me stubbornly. The breeze, which on any other day might have been refreshing, is now biting at my knuckles, turning them white. The air scrapes its way inside my lungs in shallow, unsatisfying gulps.

Back at uni, I would have laughed at this. Back then, I was knocking out 10-mile runs on a hangover, belting down city pavements in a hoodie that still smelled of someone else's flat party. There was something intoxicating about it – that mix of recklessness and momentum. I didn't need stretching routines or electrolytes or even much of a plan. I just needed noise in my ears and some thing to run from, or towards.

I thought I was strong then. But it was a different kind of strength; basically, the kind born from being too young to think my body might ever say *no* to me. I didn't appreciate what it was doing: this machine that just kept going, no matter how little sleep I gave it, or how little I fed it, or how much emotional baggage I dragged behind it. I realise now that I was an idiot.

Now, my body detects one sniffle, one irritating little cough, and decides that it would rather be in bed. A cold is hard enough, but running after a cold and with type 1 diabetes is utterly exhausting. I'd initially debated even mentioning the diabetes thing in this book, but concluded that yes, it's important. For years, I'd believed that running long distances was off-limits to me; I should wrap myself in metaphorical cotton wool, stay safe, leave it to people who had a fully-functioning pancreas. When I was diagnosed at eight years old, there were no role models that I could easily look up to, no podcasts of type 1 athletes, or type 1 influencers who normalised injecting every day and being active, or celebrities who talked about living their lives with it (e.g. Este Haim or Nick Jonas).

Yet I run because running is, in fact, a reminder of everything my body *can* still do. Alright, it's rubbish at making insulin, but with the right preparation, I can still run as far as I want. If I manage it well, I can run for hours. The problem is, of course, that diabetes doesn't always behave itself. It doesn't care if I'm two miles into a run or halfway up a mountain. It is, at best, an unpredictable and deeply annoying co-pilot. And it needs my attention *constantly.*

I check my glucose levels all the way around every run. Sometimes, the run goes well. I can treat a hypo quickly, a few Fruit Pastilles (usually sticky from being too warm in my sports bra), and I'm back in my stride. Other times, it all goes a bit sideways.

There are days when the hypos won't stop, when my legs turn to sand, my vision blurs into TV static, and I'm left shivering at the side of a road, phone in hand, waiting for someone to pick me up (this is always embarrassing). Road running at least offers an escape route in the form of a taxi, a shop or a very nice stranger with a biscuit.

Trail running is a different game entirely. Out in the wilderness, there are no corner shops and no easy rescues. If something goes wrong, it's just me, my glucose gel, and the sheep watching me, bemused. It is, at times, a little terrifying.

But it's never enough to put me off entirely. When everything is working, when the numbers hold steady and my legs feel strong, that's when I remember *exactly* why I run. Beyond that, running isn't just something I stubbornly force myself through; it actively helps. Because the secret of type 1 diabetes is that exercise, when done right, is one of the best blood sugar regulators going.

Insulin is only part of the picture. What people forget – what even doctors sometimes fail to hammer home properly – is that physical fitness changes the way your body handles glucose. Run regularly, and suddenly your insulin works better.

A good run doesn't just feel like a small win as much as a physiological reset button. It smooths out the spikes and dials down the chaos. Sometimes I run for medals, and often for endorphins, but mostly I run because it helps me cope better with the 24/7 work of type 1 diabetes.

And, I tell myself, there's probably a kind of strength in that.

★

We're in the woods now. We've run some confused loops around Caerphilly Woods car park, trying to work out which way to go while the app asks us, slightly patronisingly, whether we're going the wrong way again.

We do indeed go the wrong way twice and have so far added 1K to the route on this run (my fault entirely). I check the elevation on my app. We really haven't done that much of our estimated 378m elevation: barely even a third of it, in fact. Which, seeing as we're nearly at the end of our route, can only mean one thing: we're going up.

The route eventually takes us off the path and in between the trees. Inês is striding, strong, ahead of me, and I try to follow her pace. My legs feel like cement and the steeper the hill gets, the more my resolve wavers. Boys on mountain bikes blur past us to our left, hammering over the unsteady forest floor. We keep going. We even manage to chat between breaths, until it becomes too much and I stop on a bend in the path for a breather.

Though the setting is similar to the woods of Castell Coch, with its bare trees latticed against the sky and its thick, earthy mulch, it's far quieter. After the cyclists have disappeared, it's just us, the breeze, and our own laboured breathing. We walk for a bit. I'm mindly embarrassed for slowing my friend down. There's still another kilometre to go.

We talk about creative bursts and creative lulls. Creative seasons, if you will. One of us is in their regrowth stage creatively, letting ideas take route, immersing themselves in books. The other is writing non-stop, wringing every word out of what she knows is temporary. Now that we're older, we accept these creative seasons: the sowing of ideas, the tending, the waiting, the growing, and eventually the reaping. Just because one person is creating art non-stop doesn't mean that you never will again. You're just in different seasons.

There's something reassuring about this. It takes the pressure off in a world that wants us always on, always producing something. But that's not how nature, or creativity, works.

Sometimes a pause, and room to grow, is essential to help things bloom later.

★

We've caught a glimpse of the car park through the trees. The unmistakable, garish coral of my Fiat 500 tells me we're back. It's time, at last, for coffee.

It's cold outside, but more bearable than the clammy air inside the snack bar, thick with body heat and burger grease. Hands curled around thin polystyrene cups, we pull our jackets closer, sip, and breathe in the relief of being done.

This is the most rewarding part: the point where I'm no longer ticking off the miles or elevation, where my body is sore but satisfied, and where the warmth of coffee cuts through the chill. We don't have any more hills to climb.

Bloody lush.

A group of fresh-faced walkers sets off towards the trailhead, all bright faces and dry socks. I sip my coffee, legs heavy, and watch them go.

I mean, it wasn't a perfect run. We got lost. We slid through fields that tried to eat our shoes. I'm tired, cold, and more than a little bit worried about what state my toenails are in. But in between sips of espresso and chatter, I'm at peace, and that's all I needed from today.

Brombil Reservoir

Location
Brombil Reservoir and Margam Abbey, Port Talbot
SS 80094 86324

Distance
Approx. 10K

Parking
Margam Abbey (plenty of parking just before the car park if you don't want to get in the way of people visiting the abbey or museum).

Facilities
Toilets and lunch available at The Twelve Knights, just outside Brombil.

Tips
No matter how calm that water looks, do not swim in it. Also, bring shoes that you don't mind getting wet when crossing streams.

Brombil Reservoir

Confession: this is the second time I've tried to run this route after I messed it up spectacularly last time.

People ask me: 'How? How can you possibly get so lost in such a straightforward loop?'

Because it was me running this without a map and relying simply on common sense, is why (I might have a Master's degree, but in the common sense department, things are pretty scant).

So this time, I'm bringing company. It's a warm spring morning in March; my gloves have now been relegated to the drawer and my layers have sloughed away to just a garish leopard print running t-shirt and purple leggings (I'm not brave enough for shorts yet). As the hills loom opposite the steelworks, I'm not yet registering the difference between one side of the motorway and the other: something which I'll explain in due course but also something I'll never really fail to notice again.

Accompanying me on my run today is The Doc, someone I've known online since 2020 through Running Punks: an incredible community of misfits, music lovers, and running enthusiasts who started in Cardiff and have taken on the world through the power of social media. When I say 'the world', I mean it – today, they've got group runs all across the UK and as far as the US.

Tucking my little Fiat 500 into the side of the lane before Margam Abbey, I realise that both my running companion and I have turned up in the same shocking pink leopard print Running Punks tee.

This makes it incredibly easy to spot each other, which is an excellent thing when there's no phone signal.

Wild Running

*

The Church of St Mary, Margam Abbey is worth pointing out if you want to learn some facts to bore people with when you come here.

Before the Cistercians arrived in 1147, carved stones suggest that this was already a place of Christian worship. Robert, Earl of Gloucester, handed the land over, and the monks began working on turning it into one of the most generous Cistercian foundations in Wales.[11] And when I say generous, I mean more than just adding 15p to your Tesco self-checkout bill. When famine hit, they fed the hungry. When people were on the move, they offered shelter. And, if legend is to be believed, when the monks and locals were teetering on the edge of starvation, divine intervention arrived in the form of a mysteriously early-ripening crop, saving everyone from disaster (who needs Deliveroo?).

Margam wasn't just about food and faith, though; it was also a hub for Welsh poets, probably because we're always skint. But, like so many religious houses, its days were numbered. Henry VIII came along, decided he fancied all that monastic wealth for himself, and shut the whole operation down. Enter Sir Rice Mansel (we've encountered him before in Oxwich), who snapped up most of the estate in the 1540s and took private ownership.

Fast-forward to today and cars are swarming towards the Abbey's car park, spitting out churchgoers with arms loaded with bags. I assume there's some sort of community event happening.

I sneak a look through my sunglasses to see if I can spot any cakes.

*

The Doc grew up in Port Talbot and has a lot to tell me about what it was like, living as a young girl in an industrial South Wales town.

'It's incredibly romanticised,' she tells me as we bounce down the lane and onto a busy road, zipping where we can between cars across a busy roundabout. The air is thick with fumes and it's difficult to be heard over the sound of engines. 'You know, you hear Michael Sheen and others talking about the hardworking men of Port Talbot, but for women growing up in this town in the eighties, it was hard.' And yet 40% of the workforce in the steelworks?

Women.

That statistic almost stops me in my tracks, which isn't ideal in the middle of a busy junction. I'd never considered it. History talks so much about steel towns and their hardworking men that I'd never thought about the women keeping the works running. And yet, there they were, making up almost half the workforce; you won't see their faces on nostalgic postcards of Port Talbot, because they simply don't fit the romanticised industrial narrative of a workingman's world.

As The Doc writes in her 2021 essay, 'She was as hard as Port Talbot Steelworks but dead soft underneath', "Port Talbot is like no other steel town because of its geographical location. It is near the sea but is no 'traditional' seaside town. It has rolling hills but is not in the country. It has a famous country house built on the ruins of an Abbey, but from all these perspectives, the steelworks loom large. The coastal location of the works means that the M4 motorway connecting Port Talbot to the rest of South Wales was pushed inland. High above houses, large concrete pillars that support the motorway stride through the town, making the steelworks side of Port Talbot an island in South Wales".[12]

You'll notice this here, as I alluded to earlier. On one side of the motorway (Margam side): houses with their huge patio doors, manicured lawns and stretches of farmland. And on the side of the steelworks, terraced houses pressed close to the blaring motorway. The M4 carves straight through the middle, a boundary as physical as it is economic. It's a divide that I'll never be able to unsee.

★

We're coming into a small town now, zipping sideways into a small park. In the spring sunshine, it's busy even at ten o'clock: dogs tugging on the ends of leashes and kids flinging themselves down metal slides. For a moment, the motorway hum is swallowed by birdsong and the rustle of wind through trees.

There's a curious-looking cylindrical structure at the end of the park, which I'm informed is Beulah Calvinistic Methodist Chapel, also known locally as 'The Round Chapel', in Welsh (*Capel y Groes*).

'Round,' says Doc, 'so the devil can't hide in any corners.' There's a poem in that, surely, but it doesn't come to me today.

This chapel is a survivor, though. It was quite literally uprooted and dragged to safety when the village it belonged to was flattened to make way for the M4 in the 1970s.[13] Everything else was bulldozed, but somehow, this octagonal oddity clung on, shifting a short distance to Tollgate Park, where it now sits, admittedly looking a little out of place, but still strangely beautiful.

'I grew up opposite it,' says The Doc, pointing towards the steelworks. 'It was alive: noisy, dirty, smelly. And it shaped everything, including the way men saw themselves.' She's right. Hardness – physical, emotional – was the currency here. 'And if men were hard, women had to be soft.'

It's a story we've both heard before, even if no one ever sat us down to tell it outright.

Not just in Port Talbot, but everywhere, there's this quiet rule we learned without learning: that men had to be hard, and women had to be soft. Men held it together. Women held it all. Strength was muscle and grit; softness was sacrifice. Anything else was unacceptable, unattractive and unheard.

What we don't talk about enough is how deeply we inherit those shapes. How we carry them in our bodies. Some of us, like The Doc, grew up in the literal shadow of the steelworks: that towering, clanking metaphor for endurance and masculinity. I didn't grow up there, but I recognise the meaning of it. I know it in the way we girls are taught to apologise for our volume, our anger, our ambition, unless we could wrap it all in a soft enough tone to make it palatable.

I still do it, even now. I'm often smoothing out the edges. I'll tell the truth when I have to, but always with a polite laugh so that no one thinks I'm too much.

What does that do to a person over time? What happens when we start trimming parts of ourselves to fit someone else's idea of who we should be? It becomes not just behaviour, but identity. We start to believe we're meant to be small. Or, rather, to be manageable.

This is why running is such a release. You can't shrink on a hill and you can't apologise your way out of a steep climb. You certainly can't make yourself invisible. It asks for all of you: sweating, grunting, giving it all your effort. It brings out even the messy, loud, ferocious parts you've been taught to suppress. It's raw emotion and mental strength, and it's about being both soft and hard at the same time.

That, maybe more than anything, is what keeps pulling us back to it.

★

We're reaching a small housing estate now, just to the right from The Twelve Knights pub (make a mental note if you're fancying lunch or a drink later). Jogging past these neat little houses, it's hard to believe that just beyond them lies a TikTok-famous reservoir, a hidden splash of brilliant blue that has lured influencers and drone enthusiasts for years. Two gnomes wave at us from a perfectly trimmed lawn, their expressions frozen in either welcome or warning; I can't decide. I don't trust them. I half expect one of them to blink and whisper, "Only those with ring lights and a TikTok following may pass".

The next stretch of road is familiar. Months ago, I parked my car below the bypass, without a map, without glucose and, naturally, on par for a complete disaster. In a panic, I'd bought an orange juice on the way up and tried to squeeze it into my sports bra and failed; instead, I ended up clutching onto that with my phone in my other hand and no palms free to stop my face from hitting the mud if I fell. I'd taken every wrong turn possible, then returned here, furious.

Fortunately, The Doc knows exactly where she's going. A hush settles as the branches interlace overhead, meshing green with shade. Underfoot, the boards of a wooden bridge creak as we cross, still slick with the remnants of morning dew. Our footing is uncertain so we slow, our shoes sucked at by the deep-clogged mud. The air is thick with damp earth and leaf mulch, settling deep in the lungs, a cool relief after the tense, bracing dance of avoiding the fast, metallic blur of traffic.

The stream whispers beside us, silvered by the low light. We jog lightly over another bridge, the sound of footfall absorbed by the hush of wet wood. The trees keep us folded in, our bodies feeling less braced against the world's sharp edges.

We now have to cross the stream, and I realise this is where I went wrong last time. I didn't cross it. Instead, I went left, up a giant sodding hill and while it granted me stunning views of that brilliant blue reservoir, I was wheezing by the time I got to the top. Now, to be fair – because I'm nothing if not generous with credit where it's due – I'd also got fantastic views of the wind turbines and the steelworks from the crest of the hill, weaving in between pines and feeling the loamy ground bounce pleasingly beneath my shoes. I enjoyed that bit.

However, I'd then carried on too far right and ended up on a random farm in the arse end of nowhere and couldn't get back down. But then I made my second fatal error. I veered right, thinking I'd be clever and find a nice loop back down. Instead, I ended up near a distant farm – a nice enough little stretch of land, but where I expected no one to be around to find me save for a rusting tractor and a baffled farmer. At this point, what should have been a tidy little 5K had ballooned into a 10K odyssey through steep, ankle-breaking terrain. I'd stumble into a dead end, realise the error, and have to haul my increasingly knackered body back up the same hill, again and again. At least once – twice, if I'm being honest – I gave up entirely and just slid down half of it on my backside.

By the time I made it back down, I was furious, covered in mud, and still clutching that awkward bloody bottle of orange juice (which, by that point, I just wanted to boot into the reservoir).

There's far less drama today. The path dips, leading us down to the stream where the water ribbons through the undergrowth, silver and restless. We slow, picking our way across the uneven stepping stones, their surfaces slick with moss. The stream licks at the edges, testing the gaps. A moment's hesitation, then a leap; the stomach's brief lurch as feet land, slip and then steady.

We move onward in the right direction.

★

The path curves slightly upwards, edged by gorse and bracken, their spiced scent stirring the morning air. The reservoir remains hidden a little longer; all we can see is the sky widening above and the scrubby brown hills rising to meet them.

Brombil didn't always look like this. Years ago, thick forest surrounded the water, all shadows and deep green. Now, it's burned scrubland. Just above us, a group of teenagers scramble along the incline, hauling themselves up to the top. We briefly debate trying it, but decide it looks a little too precarious. We hope they know what they're doing.

The reservoir itself is still breathtaking: a blue so sharp and bright you have to see it for yourself. It was originally a colliery which supplied coal to the nearby copper works at Taibach, and after the colliery was closed in 1880 the mine was flooded to supply water to the docks at Port Talbot.[14] I can see why it went viral during the Covid lockdown, when we were all reconnecting with nature on our government-mandated walks outside. The water lies impossibly still, save for the faintest ripples troubling its surface, light shattering into sparkles where the wind skims across. The hills huddle close around it, their slopes mirrored in the depths. A deep inhale. My shoulders drop and I'm utterly present.

There's something quietly arresting about stumbling across natural beauty like this in a town shaped by steel, fire and noise. I mean, this is a town that wears its hardness like armour. Here, that hardness yields to the land around it. It's taking up space very quietly and very softly.

In a town that taught its people to be tough, this water is a reminder that we don't always have to be. Sometimes maybe letting the light in and reflecting it back is a sort of power in itself.

★

The stillness and sheer blue verges on mythical. It's the cyanobacteria (blue-green algae) that gives it such a distinctive colour. Intriguing though it is, it's worth pointing out that the algae can be toxic to humans and dogs, causing irritation (so do think twice about flinging yourself in). As we cross a little bridge, The Doc points to the long fronds of green weed waving beneath the surface, just waiting to snag unsuspecting ankles. It's beautiful, but not without danger.

We attempt to go right around the reservoir but today, it appears overgrown. If you want to do it, of course go ahead, but make sure you're wearing long sleeves and trousers if you want to save yourself from scratches and an onslaught of sharp brambles. We push a little farther, then decide to retreat. The Doc is in shorts. We're both in t-shirts. There's a little too much skin exposed to the elements to push all the way round.

As we circle back down to cross the stream, I'm feeling pretty chilled. There's something about being near water that soothes me, even if I am a terrible swimmer. Having grown up in Swansea, I just like knowing that it's there: the vast, rolling sweep of the bay, the reservoirs tucked into the hills, the high tides of the River Llwchwr rising to greet me every day when I walk Ted. I can be having the most stressful day imaginable, and yet, one look at that silvery crease where the water meets the sky, and something inside me relaxes a little. Not everything, of course, unless one day I toss my laptop into the estuary with Microsoft Outlook still open.

Sometimes, if I'm lucky, I can leave just a bit of the day's chaos behind me, sucked away by the tide.

On the way back, we discuss PE lessons and how much we both loathed them. About the grim predictability of it all – the whistle-blowing tyranny of netball drills, the cold misery of cross-country in the rain, and that awful hierarchy that sorted the effortlessly athletic from the rest of us (basically, the ones who lurked at the back, hoping to go unnoticed). We talk about what we are told in school: that sport is for the fast and the strong. That if you're not naturally good at it, you might as well not bother. We learned to laugh off our clumsiness and make self-deprecation a kind of armour. We told ourselves we just weren't "sporty." We believed, honestly, that our bodies weren't built for movement, for speed, or for grace.

It took me years to realise that was a lie.

So many of us, having absorbed that message early on, only come back to movement much later – tentative at first, until we realise that, actually, it feels *good*. That our bodies, despite years of being told otherwise, are more capable than we ever gave them credit for. Exercise – would you believe it – can feel joyful rather than torturous.

Hope my PE teachers are reading this, by the way.

*

By the time we're back at our cars, I'm feeling grateful. Grateful for having these gems tucked away even in the industrial parts of South Wales, and grateful for the people I've met through running. Because while it's useful to do this activity alone and get the time to think or to work through whatever chaos the week has thrown at me, there's also so much joy in company. I love those side-by-side conversations that only seem to happen when you're pushing forward together, distracting yourself from the physical effort with snatches of breathless conversation.

Sadly, there is no sign of a church cake sale, which is disappointing. I had, in a small but significant way, hoped that there would be. I had pictured a table laden with Victoria sponges, dense flapjacks and perhaps – ooh – a cheery little Bakewell tart. A small, edible reward for our morning's effort would be perfect right now. Instead, there's absolutely nothing; only the vague hum of traffic in the distance, the stretch of tarmac leading back to the day ahead.

I climb into the car, peel open a protein bar that's already halfway melted, and take a bite. It's awful. But it's okay.

I'm pretty sure there's a Jenkins bakery on the way home, anyway.

Pen-y-Fan

Location
Corn Du, Pen-y-Fan, Cribyn and Fan y Big, Brecon Beacons (or Bannau Brycheiniog, if we're being, you know, proper about it.)
SO 035173

Distance
18K

Parking
Free parking at Neuadd car park in Taf Fechan Forest.

Facilities
The Old Barn Tea Rooms are just a 2-minute drive from Taf Fechan.

Tips
Wear a woolly hat. Wear gloves. Try and go on a clear day so you can appreciate the astounding views and not feel like the main character in PS1 Silent Hill.

Pen-y-Fan

You know those runs that you utterly detest in the moment, but at the end they make you feel like an absolute hero? This is the boss level of all the runs in this book. This is the one that will build your character, test your mentality, and challenge your thighs to the extreme. And it's the one that will stun you with how beautiful Wales really is.

The Corn Du, Pen y Fan, Cribyn and Fan y Big loop is spectacularly, beautifully and horribly brutal. It's essentially a really long assault on your legs, disguised as a scenic jaunt through the Brecon Beacons' finest ridgelines.

And I have decided that this is how I will be spending my day. (In my defence, I had no idea that we'd be running to the peak of the highest mountain in South Wales at all; Inês and I were simply sent a route to follow, which we did. Never trust the recommendations of hardcore trail runners.)

*

Jeff Buckley is wailing about heartbreak, the car speakers trembling with the raw agony of 'Lover, You Should Have Come Over', and then makes way for abruptly heavy metal, drums rattling the dashboard like a tiny earthquake. Outside, the road snakes around a stunning, glassy reservoir and we're almost headbanging over potholes on our way to Taf Fechan Forest. Our bags are loaded with fresh pastries; a slight miscommunication means that we both took on the snack-buying responsibility and have enough butter croissants and cinnamon swirls to feed Brecon's population for the next week.

The cold wind whistles through the gaps in the car window. It's going to be a fresh one. Inês is in charge of the navigation, which means that we will not end up in some obscure part of the country, miles away from where we need to be.

I step out of the car and immediately regret not wearing more layers. It's early, and the air has teeth: sharp little pinpricks of cold against my face. Having guzzled half a litre of water on the drive, I become painfully aware of how tight my bladder feels. I excuse myself and nip behind a tree, only to somehow manage to pee all over my brand-new trail shoes.

*

It's a gentle incline through Taf Fechan Forest. We're going at a steady pace, our strides short, and my pigtails bouncing under my woolly hat (my mother, whenever she sees me like this post-run, asks me why I am dressed like a child). This feels fine so far. This might, I think, be an okay run today.

Inês points out the upcoming elevation on her phone and I realise that I am very much wrong.

There's a sharp turn right and we continue running uphill. To our left, thick pines pierce the mist, the mountains dark behind them. This feels gentle, easy enough, and I'm overconfident. What I don't realise is that the huge mountain to our left is more than a scenic backdrop and is, in fact, what we'll be cresting the summit of. Pushing our way through the gate, we see a bridge below us over Lower Neuadd Reservoir, a shimmering white ribbon that cuts through the mountains and rushes below us. Where the light catches, the water flares gold, then vanishes, pulled back into the cool, quiet rush.

We cross the bridge and it's time to go up.

And up. And up some more. I stop to catch my breath and try to regain feeling in my calves, then push on with the ascent. The stunning backdrop behind me lowers into mist the farther we climb. The ridges left in the grass from the many people who've climbed before us are spaced wide apart, so every step feels like I'm hauling myself from one leg to the other.

I'm bloody knackered already.

Several people pass us, heading the other way, which concerns me. Have we done this the wrong way round? We were given a circular route but it never told us *which* direction we were supposed to run in.

I'm not thinking of writing or anything creative at all at this point, by the way. Most of my mental capacity is taken up by telling myself to just keep moving, to somehow push through the burn that's accumulating in my calves. Inês, who is still far more adept at hills and navigating tricky climbs than I am, mutters to herself to keep going in a soothing Portuguese accent. It is not long before she is giving me a crash course in Portuguese swear words.

The climb to the Craig Fan Du ridge is a steep 1km.

A young woman coming towards us emits a high-pitched yelp, her feet skidding beneath her, arms flailing like an inflatable tube man in a hurricane. She declares loudly that she thinks she's done this the wrong way round. This is deeply reassuring for us. But I think, no matter which way you do this run, you're going to have to face a steep ascent anyway. Sadly, there's no way to cheat the mountains.

The mist becomes thicker, obscuring the valley below, so there's no longer any point in stopping to take photographs (or pretend to, if only to catch my breath). There's a wooden fence we reach out to grip, which has tilted almost horizontally outwards from all the other hikers and runners clinging to it over time. A thin sheen of ice clings to a warning sign. Whatever it's telling us, we probably already know.

By now, frost is beginning to form on our woolly hats like crusted salt. We eventually agree to slow to a walk to the summit; the quad-burn and the face-freeze is too much. The path clambers, a restless muscle of earth and stone, twisting its spine towards the sky. The rock face is sheer and slippery; years of climbing having left the land peeled open to the icy winds. It's eerie, muffled and close, my breath a small ghost in the frozen air. We stop, stretch and breathe deeply.

Filling the lungs is tough to do up here (that's my excuse, anyway).

We take a right. The earth is wet and cold beneath my feet, but I don't care. I'm just relieved not to still be climbing steeply upwards. That's not to say there's no incline however because there absolutely is, but it's gradual. I quickly glance at my insulin pump to see what my blood sugar readings are (hard efforts can sometimes trigger a glycogen dump, sending my blood sugar skyward). The cold has decided to throw a spanner in the works; the continuous glucose monitor in my arm has stopped working in the cold temperatures and a curt error message flashes at me: *Lost sensor signal*. I cancel it with a sigh. Fortunately for me, there's an old-school blood glucose meter squeezed into my pocket for emergencies.

I crouch on the dark rock, icy wind battering my face. A quick finger prick, a squeeze, and the blood comes easily, which is no surprise, given my heart is currently attempting to launch itself out of my ribcage. We still have 12K to go, so I'm hoping for a slightly elevated reading rather than having to battle an oncoming hypoglycaemic episode at this point.

11.8mmol. Slightly high, which is expected given the physical exertion we've just pushed ourselves through, but that's fine. It'll come down quickly over the course of the run, as my heart rate drops on more level terrain. And if I do go hypo in the next 12K, my pockets are straining with packets of Clif Bloks. This is in addition to the two packets of Fruit Pastilles stuffed down either side of my bra.

If nothing, I'm determined to go down chewing.

★

I realise, at this point, how much a good view keeps me going because right now, there isn't one. And it's *tough*. With previous runs, an uphill section has always meant a guaranteed reward of a stunning, sweeping view of the Welsh landscape. I always look forward to something that can stop me in my tracks and makes me feel utterly present.

Not here, though. We should be enjoying some of the most breathtaking views in all of Wales, but we've come on a day that's so overcast that there's little more to look at than rock, mist, and the loping silhouettes of knackered hikers ahead of us. I'd like to return to this (I think, once my legs have recovered) on an early morning in summer, or in the height of spring, where the views can really give me a sense of reward for the monumental effort it takes to keep running in these conditions.

For now, my only reward is a rock-solid Fruit Pastille, fished from my bra like a sparkling pebble, a little while later as my sugars start dropping.

The ice gets thicker. The incline gets steeper. And, naturally, running becomes more challenging. Inês is way ahead of me, her footwork deft over the glittering ice and pools of water. I try to keep up but it's not long before I make my first slip and someone behind me catches my elbow: a kind woman in a thick purple hiking jacket, effectively stopping me from slipping onto my face.

I thank her. All of my teeth are fortunately still fortunately intact.

*

This ridgeline carries on for 3.5km. The cold is vicious. It sinks its teeth in and shakes – a bit like Ted when he's got hold of one of my compression socks. Eventually, we spot a line of people, shifting from foot to foot and looking strangely overjoyed to be standing up here in the cold. At the front, they take turns grinning beside what appears to be, at best, an unremarkable rock. I turn to Inês, baffled. She points at the sign: *Pen y Fan*.

2,907ft of elevation later, we've somehow summited the highest peak in South Wales entirely by accident.

We opt out of joining the queue. We're both wondering how many of those photographs are going to end up as Tinder profile pictures.

Instead, we snap a quick selfie with nothing behind us but snow and rock, our hats crusted with frost and cheeks pinched red by the wind. In the photograph, there's somehow no trace of the exhaustion in our faces, and no hint of the fact that our shoes have quietly transformed into small, portable reservoirs of ice water. What we're feeling isn't euphoria, but more a mixture of surprise with a trace of very slight smugness. Despite living in Wales for all of my life, I've never actually visited this place at all.

Pen y Fan, along with its slightly shorter but no less dramatic sibling, Corn Du, was once known as *Cadair Arthur*: Arthur's Chair. The name alone evokes an image of the legendary king lounging at the summit, surveying his kingdom with a goblet of something potent and delicious (which I probably need right now). Sadly, history doesn't back this up. There's no evidence of a sword plunged into a stone and no knights galloping up the ridge. Instead, local legend offers a tale of Arthur taking on a gang of unruly wild boars, slaying their leader, and sending its carcass rolling down into what is now the *Afon Twrch*: the River of the Boar.

So basically, this was more about pest control.

Today, Pen y Fan's real claim to fame is as the proving ground for the UK Special Forces. The infamous Fan Dance – a 24km slog through the mountains – serves as an early test of fitness, navigation, and unbelievable endurance. Hopeful recruits must haul an 18kg backpack, a 5kg rifle, and a water bottle up these mountains.

I want to sleep on a rock just thinking about it.

★

Finally, we begin to descend. You know that euphoric sensation when you've been desperate for a pee for hours, and then, finally, relief washes through you, leaving nothing but bliss in its wake? It's kind of like that. But in my calves. They've spent most of this run clenched, furious and tight; now, at last, they begin to release. It's heavenly, but it's short-lived.

Because, of course, what goes down must go back up when you're in between mountains. We reach the saddle between Pen y Fan and Cribyn, only to realise that yet another climb awaits us; this one apparently worth it for incredible views. Except, thanks to the unrelenting fog, those views remain an abstract concept.

'Oh, for God's *sake*,' I mutter, reaching the summit. I am so bored of mist.

It's not long before we have to slow to a walk again. In trail running, this is quite refreshingly acceptable because the terrain dictates the terms. If it's steep enough, rocky enough, or punishing enough, you walk. There's no shame to that. You're free to do whatever nature tells you to.

I have no idea what my pace is at this point. I glance at my watch, but it only gives me elapsed time and distance, and I'm too cold, too tired, and too mathematically incompetent to work it out. Which, in itself, is freeing. Today is all about surrendering and going with it, however I can.

This saddle is boggy, so be prepared. Pack spare socks and a change of shoes to leave in the car; your shrivelled toes will thank you for it. Our feet plunge into freezing pools and I wish I'd worn better socks than the £3 Disney ones from Primark I'd fished from my drawer in the dark this morning. We clamber up, pressing our hands to the damp rocks to steady ourselves. Progress is slow.

Cribyn stands at 2508ft, so it's no small feat either. The fog is so thick, it's like looking down into a pool of milk.

> *Below, the sky offers nothing but smoky cloud,*
> *its valleys swallowed entirely: raw, bright, untranslatable.*

Some inspiration at last. If I can't see anything, I can at least try to create something out of nothing.

★

The whole time we're running, Inês and I frequently turn our necks to check if the other is still there, depending on who's ahead. As a woman, you barely even realise anymore that you do it automatically. It's a given that you'll look over your shoulder often; either for your running companion or for someone that might be following you.

This might sound a bit dramatic. It's not. And I wish this wasn't the case.

Between 17 December 2022 - 6 January 2023, Adidas commissioned international research surveying 9,000 people (4,500 who identify as women and 4,500 who identify as men) across Japan, China, US, UK, Mexico, UAE, France, Germany, and South Korea, aged 16-34. The findings revealed that 92% of women reported feeling concerned for their safety, with half (51%) afraid of being physically attacked, compared to 28% of men. Over a third (38%) of women have experienced physical or verbal harassment, and of these women over half have received unwanted attention (56%), sexist comments or unwanted sexual attention (55%), been honked at (53%), or followed (50%).[15]

There's not a single woman I know who also runs that hasn't felt unsafe at some point while running. There have been times where I've been shouted at out of cars or from the side of the road by groups of men. There was that time I had to change my regular running route because a man started appearing in the same spot to watch and shout at me while I was doing my interval training. And it doesn't just happen in the running space either; I once had to email a yoga teacher to report a man who kept moving his hand onto me during the class. I was too anxious to ever go back.

For many women, the darker nights in winter don't just bring a drop in temperature but a drop in freedom. We adjust out plans, reconsider our routes, and the simple act of stepping outside for a run becomes a calculation of risk versus reward. And I hate that this is our reality.

It forces some into a compromise: switching to a treadmill in a stuffy, overlit gym or, worse, hanging up their running shoes entirely until the clocks leap forward again. And so, when the London Marathon announced its return to its usual April slot, after its brief pandemic-induced autumn run, it wasn't just an adjustment to the race calendar. It was, by many women, seen as a sentence: months of training through the cold, in the dark, in conditions that for many men are merely inconvenient but for many women are downright dangerous.

We don't care so much about the weather as we do about the knot in our stomachs when we realise the path ahead is empty. There's the instinctive check over the shoulder. The keys in the fist. The endless calculations of where is safe, when is safe, and whether safe enough is ever actually safe at all.

It's why organisations such as White Ribbon UK are on a mission to educate and encourage men to challenge this issue and become allies, every day, to stop violence against women and girls before it starts.[16]

Because everyone, everywhere deserves an equal right to enjoy running without fear. But we still have such a long way to go.

★

From the summit of Cribyn, the ridgeline draws us onwards, leading south-east in a long, teasing descent away from Pen-y-Fan. I'm just starting to enjoy the ease of this when there's a final, brutal drop down to 'The Gap' – a broad, gravel-bruised bridleway that cleaves the space between Cribyn and Fan y Big.

Now, you've got a decision to make here. If you want to do the traditional 'Horseshoe' route, turn back down towards the Neuadd Reservoir. However, this isn't the route we've been sent today so we're going to push upwards one last time. On a clear day (yes, you've guessed it), you'll get incredible views.

Pushing our way through the mist, we're just doing it for punishment at this point. Hello again, fog.

Fan y Big is a short, sharp ascent that leads to the summit, where we are supposed to be rewarded with panoramic views and, more importantly, one of the most photographed rocks in Wales: the stone 'diving board.' Perched dramatically over the valley below, it's an irresistible platform for hikers and runners to strike a triumphant pose: legs braced, arms wide, the wind howling dramatically as though we've just reached the crest of Mount Mordor.

We do not take a photo on the diving board today, mainly because we can't see how far down we'll crash if we mess up our footing (which, in this howling wind, isn't an impossibility).

We don't get the photo. And weirdly, that feels absolutely fine. Somewhere along the way, we've become obsessed with proof, and making sure the world sees the thing we did – whether that's the summit we reached, the miles we ran or the places we've visited. Visibility has become currency. It's not enough to climb the mountain. You have to document it, curate it and caption it now. But what does it mean to reach the top and not show anyone?

Fan y Big offers nothing today except a slab of rock somewhere in the fog and two women standing in the cold, soaked to the skin, but still, somehow, happy. There's a ridiculous satisfaction in reaching somewhere no one can see and knowing we got there anyway. Even if I did post the view, it's very unlikely people would have cared anyway, scrolling their phones over their cornflakes.

Now, finally, it is time to go all the way down.

I fall several times. The trail is a treacherous mix of mud, ice and wet grass. It looks almost designed for me to grab a sheet of cardboard and toboggan my way down like a small child. I don't have cardboard, and I am, of course, a serious runner, so I instead do the boring thing and test the effectiveness of my trail shoes.

'I think I need new shoes again,' I announce, just as I lose my footing and land flat on my arse, flinging a satisfying arc of mud onto the poor unsuspecting walkers beside me. They say nothing. A man wipes his face.

The path back into the woods is easier, but still requires some technical footwork. We bounce awkwardly between grass ridges and loose rock, our ankles catching just often enough to elicit a steady stream of swearing, half in English, half in Portuguese. A group of walkers ahead of us steps politely aside as we lurch past, chaotic.

'Fair play, running this!' one of them says.

I inform him it's a poor decision on my part, then slip on a rock to prove it.

★

The crunch of gravel beneath our heels tells us we're nearing the end, edging back full circle into Taf Fechan Forest. Ice still glitters in our knitted hats, our strides heavy, and our stomachs growling. We remind each other every two minutes that we're getting closer to our bag of pastries.

This stretch is short, but when your legs ache this much, it feels like you've been running for three centuries.

My watch hits 18K and I see the car appear into view. We've been wise enough to park next to a bench, granting us the relief of sitting down instead of crumpling onto the tarmac like limp puppets.

Inês shakes her head. She somehow has another 0.1km to complete from pausing her watch earlier, so she starts running tiny, determined loops behind the car, her eyes fixed on the numbers. Round numbers are inexplicably, infuriatingly important to runners.

We glug on cold water and breathe deeply. The pastries are no longer warm, but I take out the bag anyway and drop them onto the table like valuable spoils.

It's just a supermarket pastry. A mass-produced, probably additive-loaded all-butter croissant that once sat in a uniform row under the slightly mournful glow of the in-store bakery lights. And yet, after miles of wind-whipped ridgelines, of slipping, scrambling, and swearing, it might as well have been hand-delivered from the best pastry chef in Paris.

I tear off a corner, letting it collapse in my mouth into soft, buttery layers.

I mean, there was no finish line ribbon fluttering in the wind. And we didn't get any stunning views. But we got the story. And as we sit there, tearing pastry in our teeth, flakes snowing over our running jackets, that'll do for today.

Ogmore-by-Sea

Location
Ogmore-by-Sea, Vale of Glamorgan
SS 88185 73478

Distance
11K (long enough to feel like it was a good effort, but short enough not to have to nap for the rest of the day).

Parking
Ogmore Rivermouth Car Park is very reasonably priced, but there are plenty of other car parks along the route too.

Facilities
The Welsh Coffee Co is just up the road, serving up strong coffee and incredible coastal views. Public toilets at St Brides Major and conveniently placed pubs along the way. (For the landscape, not necessarily for you). Please also note the warm cinnamon swirls at The Welsh Coffee Co.
They taste every bit as good as they smell.

Ogmore-by-Sea

A coastal run in winter means I expect to lean into the wind, to pull my hood tight against the sting of rain, and watch the sea heave itself into furious peaks. I'm a pro at that by now.

Not today, though. February, but only just, and the air has lost its bite, turned soft at the edges, like butter left out too long. Below, the sea muscles over the shore, all froth and swagger. It's the first morning that carries a hint of spring and I want to taste it by the spoonful.

It's 8am and Inês and I are the first people in the car park. The sky is a clean, poured-out blue. The breeze is cool on my skin, gentle enough that the ridiculously thick gloves feel like overkill, along with the thick woolly hat. I've come along dressed like I'm going for a week in the Alps, not a jog in South Wales.

The trails are waiting and each time I do it, it feels like an end-of-week treat. Throughout the week, I've been hammering out the usual 10K route around the roads in North Gower, which while picturesque, is pretty brutal on my knees. I can feel the twinge of shin splints starting and since writing this book and making trails a bigger part of my routine, my body and mind have thanked me. Finishing a road run is nice, sure, but it just doesn't beat that feeling of finally seeing the car when your quads are burning, you're covered in mud, and you know there's a hot coffee just minutes away. Trail running, strangely, is becoming something of a therapy for me, particularly as a self-confessed overthinker.

The start of the run hugs close to the coastline, giving us sweeping views of the sea below. Although it doesn't feel windy, the waves are breaking far from the shoreline in thin, creamy folds. The light keeps shifting: one moment dazzling, scattering off the sea in a thousand bright splinters, and the next soft, slipping behind a slow-moving cloud.

For now, the run is easy. The coastline curves ahead, rising and falling ever so gently, like the landscape is drawing breath. A couple of runners pass us with wide smiles and wish us a good morning. Everyone, it seems, is relieved to experience an early taste of the coming spring.

I appreciate an early morning weekend run, even if the early alarm initially makes me want to throw my phone at the wall and retreat deeper into the duvet. I'm out before the roads get busy, and the Whatsapp group messages start pinging about weekend plans, and I realise I need to go to the bloody shop again (why, every day, must there always be a reason to go to the shop?). The air still feels unclaimed, the light fresh. Just ahead, there's a woman in a turquoise coat walking a collie and just beyond her, a man leaning against a gate with a flask in hand, watching the morning sun leak across the sky. They nod in greeting, silently understanding the quiet joy of being outside before the world is out of its pyjamas.

★

The map on my phone tells us to head left, which means we leave the sea behind us and push ourselves up a grassy hill, which after days of rain, is more slippery than it looks. It's short and sharp; we're both determined to get to the top without stopping. By the time we crest the summit, breath coming in short, surprised bursts, I glance at the map again and realise, of course, we've overshot (I'm in charge of navigation, unfortunately). We were meant to turn right along the coastal path. The one that would have kept us blissfully level and not clawing our way all the way to the top of a sodden incline.

Which is fine. Absolutely fine. Between these trail runs and my PT sessions, my quads are, I think, approaching superhuman status. I already can't wait for the next time I'm drunk enough to threaten to squat a bouncer.

The sea below us has power in its movement; the foam sprays aggressively over black rocks, so slick they look almost oiled. In the distance, four women, wrapped in blindingly bright towels, stand laughing, rubbing warmth back into their limbs after a baltic swim. They are far braver than I am. Wild swimmers are people I'm envious of, but not committed enough to ever join in with. I've tried. I've entertained the idea many times, mainly in summer: a sticky day in mid-July, running along the coast, where I'll finally plunge into cold water and work my muscles against the tide, letting the salt soothe my skin.

But when it comes down to it, I simply dip my toe cautiously into the water, shriek, and turn back to go and mope on the sand. My friend Roisin swears by sea swimming, even in November. There was one morning in Folkestone, in mid-July, where she took me to the beach at 7am after some particularly raucous birthday celebrations and swore this would fix my headache. She pushed through the water gracefully, barely flinching at the cold.

I got up to my waist and started turning blue. I opted for espresso and dark sunglasses, and refused to go in again.

*

The coastal path becomes muddy. Even though a downhill stretch is always welcome, it can also be precarious; our trail shoes are fully put to the test as we slide down to the car park at St Bride's. It's here I should pause to note something of critical importance to runners: there's a reassuring number of public toilets on this route. And if you're a runner – a real runner – you'll know why this matters. Because no matter how sleek your Garmin, how expensive your carbon-plated shoes, or how religiously you've followed your training plan, there is one inescapable truth about this sport: runner's belly eventually gets us all. One day, mid-run, your stomach will turn on you.

It'll start as a mild cramping, or maybe just a vague unease. Then, suddenly, it's a situation. Then there's the frantic scanning of your surroundings, and the desperate calculations of how far you are from civilisation versus how much time you realistically have. If you're lucky, a public toilet will present itself and you'll throw yourself through the doors in the hope that today they are unlocked.

If they're not, then let's just say, you haven't truly lived as a runner until you've crouched behind a hedge, praying that the leaves are both soft and non-toxic.

★

We're steering away from the coast now and into the woods. We pass a charming, stone-coloured cottage, so gorgeously picturesque it might as well come with a resident family of Sylvanian squirrels tending a miniature vegetable patch. We find ourselves idly fantasising about living in one, about growing unruly honeysuckle and stacking logs for a fire that would burn all through winter. We would make bread. We would own a whittling knife, even if neither of us has a clue how to use one. We would give up our tec careers to pick carrots.

The trees thicken as we press further into the woodland and the light filters through in sheets of gold, catching in the leaves, splashing onto the path in broken, burnished fragments. At last, it feels as though winter is nowhere to be seen. We can pretend it's not February and actually believe it. We both agree that it's been a very long winter, particularly so for Inês, who grew up accustomed to balmy afternoons in Lisbon.

Some people love winter running. Some people revel in the rush of cold air in their lungs, the bite of rain against their skin, the satisfying crunch of frozen mud beneath their feet. They insist it makes them feel alive, and that there is something elemental, or almost spiritual, about tearing through the landscape in conditions that most people avoid. Perhaps you are one of these runners. If so, I admire you. I want to be like you.

I want to be the person who bounds joyfully through driving rain, pushing into the wind, rather than the person who complains all the way through the downpours, fantasising about a hot bath glutted with Radox. But if I'm honest, I thrive best in late summer or early autumn, where the morning light spreads itself over the field like warm honey, and where the air is sticky with the scent of damp earth and overripe berries. I like those summer runs where you sweat, not because you're fighting against the elements, but because the tarmac is shimmering, exhaling the last of its summer warmth before the slow decline into colder days.

Even so, there's something gorgeous about this unusually bright February morning, this stripped-back, bare-boned landscape of winter. Running these trails now, when the trees are skeletal and the earth is slick, I'm starting to appreciate it in a way I never have before. There's the sharpness of it, and the way the wind cuts clean through the land, uncluttered by the fullness of summer foliage. Maybe it takes running in the deep, raw cold to truly understand the beauty of warmth. Maybe you need to see the land stripped back to a thin shadow of itself to really appreciate the first signs of spring: the first bud, or the first fat, brown rabbit.

Or, perhaps, the first day you step outside and realise that actually, you can finally leave your gloves at home.

This trail continues to surprise me with its variety. We climb uphill through the woods and reach a stone stile that takes us into farmland. The ground becomes boggy, a green expanse that swallows every step with a wet suck. Within moments, our run has turned into something resembling an elaborate, mud-drenched high-knee drill, as we attempt to navigate the field without disappearing into the earth like those cartoon characters that always seem to vanish into quicksand.

It's warm now, the sun pressing down, the air thick with the scent of damp grass and livestock. In the distance, a farmer yells. At first, it's just a distant, indecipherable holler, but then it becomes louder and more frenzied (I think). He is herding his sheep, shifting them across the land. For a brief, bizarre second, I wonder if we have stumbled upon some rural rave, like some underground barn party where the bass is just the heavy thud of hooves against the mud.

If so, I really hope I'm invited.

It's just everyday farm life, though. It's a normal, everyday rhythm for the people who live here, yet to me it feels almost theatrical. And now, instead of being a tranquil observer, I'm actively ruining it by flailing across the field like a distressed chicken, slipping every few steps, with my arms pinwheeling.

We flail together gracelessly through the field, aiming for the next stile in mud-splattered leggings.

It's onto the road after this, which both of us are mildly disappointed about. We're sad to find that the soft give of earth, the thrill of uncertain footing, and the cartoon-like plop of a shoe nearly sucked off by mud are now all replaced with grey, predictable pavement. Worse still, the tarmac is just smooth enough to remind us of something trail runners rarely speak of outside hushed, supportive circles: the horrible design flaw that is the modern sports bra.

We try to adjust our straps and stretch the elastic; do that awkward half-shrug, half-pull motion that never works but at least makes us feel like we're trying. We both grumble, shifting the fabric about pointlessly and wincing at the first hints of chafing that will, without intervention, become bloody unbearable by the time we're finished.

If you're planning on stopping on the route, the first pub is here: The Farmer's Arms. We don't stop there today (it's early morning and we decide a pint of bitter isn't the healthiest breakfast option), so we move on, winding our way through the charming little village. It's familiar. I've been here before, I realise, though last time was on two wheels: a 50-mile charity cycle from Cardiff to Swansea. I remember this stretch well, mostly because at this exact point in the ride, I'd actually considered calling it a day and veering straight into the local Greek restaurant instead.

Ogmore-by-Sea

★

There's a sign for a church and we turn left to pass it I resist stopping Inês to explore it; we still have 5K to go. It's all uphill and on tarmac from here, which we are both very unhappy about (or our knees are, at least). So unhappy, in fact, that we give up a little way from the top and walk until the tarmac gives way to earth and grass once again. In front of us, there are forked paths curving out over the grass. We follow the path on our left and push on.

There's not much I can tell you about this section of the trail, only that it goes on for quite a bit without much happening. I even remark to Inês that I'm getting a bit bored here and am missing the sea, and hopping over roots, and even the chance of cows.

You know, there are periods of writing this book that have felt the same. I've gone along tracks that led nowhere, then deleted an entire chapter. I've bored myself with descriptions that don't convey what I want to say. Everyone talks about the rush of the beginning, when the thrill of a new idea grips you, and words start pouring out faster than you can catch them. And then there's the satisfaction of the final paragraph, in that moment when the entire thing feels like it clicks into place at last (at least, until you read the whole thing back through and decide you want to start again because you hate it). And, oh, the sense of *relief*. I've seen plenty of social media posts of laptops and champagne, 'The End' typed out across the screen. I've seen plenty of book launch celebrations or read excited posts about new book projects.

But no one talks much about the bit in the middle. This is the long, slow stretch where the novelty has worn off and the finish line's too far away to see. You keep going, but you don't feel particularly inspired. You just put one foot (or word) in front of the other and hope it leads somewhere. Sometimes you're on a roll and things flow.

Sometimes you hit dead end after dead end.

This part of the run has the same energy. We're on that mostly unglamorous part where the path refuses to reveal anything new. When running trails, you have to learn not to quit just because the high has worn off. Sometimes, it's best just to stick with the boredom because eventually, the terrain will change. A new view might open up, and an unexpected twist in your story lands, so long as you keep moving long enough to reach it.

And this is what we do now. We keep going until we have to follow a little path through the trees, hoping for something exciting to appear on the other side.

★

We nearly get taken out by golf balls. Again.

For five whole minutes, we crouch, watching a line of polo-shirted golfers swing, full-force, at the balls. We try to wave to a woman at the end of the line of golfers to indicate our presence. She sees us, but takes a while to let everyone know that they could possibly knock us out.

We hover, awkwardly, feeling mildly embarrassed. Do we shout? Do we wave our arms? Do we just leg it and risk everything?

Eventually, we are waved past and out to safety. These routes really need to stop crossing golf tournaments.

The next part is all tangles of gorse, brambles, and a winding path of slippery gulleys. The water in between these ridges is ankle-deep, so to navigate this, we end up with our feet either side of the ridges and the water in between us, trying not to fall or do the splits.

I didn't turn up to yoga this week. Again. So I suppose this makes up for it.

In some parts, we simply have to admit defeat and allow our feet to plunge into the muddy water. And once your feet are cold, that's it; it's inevitable that you're going to shiver until you reach a steaming hot shower. I am about a fifty-minute drive away from mine, however.

There's a buzzing sound somewhere in the depths of my sports bra and I realise my insulin pump is alerting me to a hypo. The thing with trail running is that it's easy to assume that the weak legs and dizzy head are because you've just thrown yourself up a hill, so it can be easy to miss the signs of your blood sugars plunging low. Had I felt like this in a boardroom or in the middle of Tesco then I'd know, immediately, what was happening.

But it's so much harder to tell when you're covered in mud and exhausted from running. I suddenly realise that the pins and needles spreading up my legs and the numbness setting into my tongue makes sense. Clif Bloks to the rescue.

Normally I'd stop and let my blood sugars rise before continuing, but we're so close to the end and I'm only just on the cusp of a hypo, so I continue. I monitor it closely, my feet plunging into cold water every time I glance at my pump.

At times, buzzing, beeping, and responding accordingly, I feel not all that different from a Tamagotchi.

★

Ogmore Castle comes into view on our right. There are no towering battlements shoving at the sky and no fairytale turrets demanding attention (unlike the lovely Castell Coch). Instead, it sits, half-crumbled but hauntingly beautiful in the morning sunlight beside the River Ogmore.

Ogmore is one of three castles – along with Coity and Newcastle – built to guard the Norman frontier against the Welsh-held west. In the twelfth century, little more than earth and wood, it was hurried into existence by men who knew this land was not yet theirs to keep. The stone came later, and by the thirteenth century, the curtain wall had risen too.[17]

What's striking about Ogmore isn't what's been restored, but what's actually been left alone. All we see are skeletal walls and the grass curling quietly through the cracks, as if nature is reclaiming it slowly, inch by inch. The earliest defences – the ridges and the ditches – haven't been swallowed by the earth.

The deep ditch around the inner ward, designed to flood with seawater at high tide, still curves around the ruins. It's not a castle of conquest anymore, nor a symbol of power or defence. The walls lean into their own collapse, fringed with grass, and all that's left is this steadfast grey rock. Some places just endure.

The river that twists alongside it is a brilliant blue today. Across its banks, strong women in helmets lean forward, mounted upon horses, gathering speed; their horses all heat and muscle. Their hooves thud against the earth and I find myself wondering why I don't see more of this outside of period dramas. It's not long before our feet start sliding over pebbles and we slow down to a stop, deciding to walk off the end of our run rather than risk tripping over, face-first into a rockpool.

Inês seems absorbed in searching through pebbles, stopping every now and then to turn one in her hand.

'I just really like rocks,' she says, filling her pockets. She points out, helpfully, that you can make a decent ashtray from the right one.

We spend a while there, appreciating bloody good stones.

★

We decide to refuel at The Welsh Coffee Co., just half a mile up the road. The café is perched up high, offering a sweeping panorama of the sea rolling and crumpling against the rocks, its surface oscillating between blue to steel, depending on the whim of the sun. The air is thick with the tang of salt, the deep warmth of ground coffee, and the scent of something sweet and cinnamon-laced emerging from an oven. My stomach growls.

We weave our way between families refuelling on hot lattes and toasted sandwiches, elderly couples sitting in the comfortable silence of decades spent together, and cyclists methodically inhaling calories while leaning on their bikes.

Beside us, a toddler – bundled into a coat at least two sizes too big – is making a joyful circuit of the café. His tiny feet slap against the floor with wild determination, arms swinging like uncoordinated windmills, and his cheeks flushed from the effort. He stumbles, rights himself with a wobble, and takes off again, giggling with the kind of unfiltered delight I only ever see in children and dogs.

The beautiful thing about watching this is that he's not running for fitness, or to clear his head, or to burn off breakfast. He's not measuring splits or tracking progress. He's not thinking about how he looks, or how far he's gone, or whether it 'counts'. He's running simply because he can, and because it feels good.

Movement is the most natural language his little body knows how to speak right now. The funny thing is that at some point, we forget that. Somewhere along the line, movement becomes a means to an end, whether that's a punishment, a metric, or a thing to optimise. We lose the instinct for running as *play*, as exploration, or as pure, useless joy. It all becomes very serious and scheduled. I think that's what these trail runs are slowly giving back to me: that sense of uncomplicated motion. It's nice, simply letting my body take the lead again, and relearning how to run not to get somewhere, but to feel something.

The toddler barrels past again, arms out like a plane. For a moment, I wish I had his energy. But more than that, I want his freedom. Imagine that: giving yourself full permission to just move because it feels right. Imagine you could forget everything else and just go, without worrying what other people think of you.

Even so, I'm not tempted to run circles around the café while squealing, but it's nice to imagine I could if I really wanted to.

The subject of road races comes up while we sip our coffees. I say that I'm not signing up for road races anytime soon. The urge to pin a number to my chest and pound tarmac until my knees threaten to pop has long since faded, and the thought of reaching a start line before 9am in a massive crowd makes me want to hide up a tree.

As long as there are trails to follow, hills to climb, and paths that disappear into the trees before spitting me out somewhere new, I'll be lacing up my shoes and chasing after these chaotic routes instead.

Perhaps the answer is to approach it like an excited toddler let loose.

Top: past the Point, Oxwich Bay
Bottom: Oxwich Castle (well. Manor, really…)

Top: distant view of the iconic Three Cliffs
Bottom: Pennard Pill. Very fun stones to jump on

Pennard Castle. Watch out for golf balls

Castell Coch. Wouldn't look out of place in Disneyland

Caerphilly Mountain. Run "caerphilly" over the muddy descents

Brombil Reservoir. Unbelievably blue

Top: ascent to Pen-y-Fan. Sympathies to your calf muscles
Middle: view over the Lower Neuadd Reservoir
Bottom: beautiful Brecon. If you see this, you've made it back down

Top: Ogmore-by-Sea. We are definitely By Sea
Bottom: wild swimmers at Ogmore. You shiver looking at them

Merthyr Mawr: popular training spot for Olympic athletes

Salmon Leaps, minus any leaping salmon

King Arthur's Stone, Cefn Bryn. Apparently this fitted in Arthur's shoe

St Illtud's Church, Llantwit Major

St Donat's College entrance, Llantwit Major
Once home to star-studded parties

Waterfall, Pen Pych. Perfect place to take a breather

Tintern Abbey. As majestic as you can get

Top: onto Marsh Road from Crofty
Middle: view over estuary, Crofty
Bottom: neigh-bours in Llanrhidian

Merthyr Mawr

Location
Merthyr Mawr Warren Nature Reserve, Bridgend
SS 83773 76979

Distance
11K

Parking
Newton Beach Car Park (note that there is a small fee).

Facilities
Two pubs near the car park: The Ancient Briton and Jolly Sailor.

Tips
Go there late morning to early afternoon so there's an excuse for lunch and a cold glass of something refreshing afterwards.

Merthyr Mawr

A Friday morning off and the sunshine is glorious, so today I'm taking (read: dragging) Ian along with me to Merthyr Mawr Warren Nature Reserve. Joining us today is our friend Matt, who is probably the fastest trail and fell runner I know; he's a runner whose legs that don't seem to acknowledge the concept of exhaustion. This means two things: first, that I'll be spending a lot of time watching his back disappear into the distance, and second, that I'll have to work hard to disguise the fact that running on sand is exhausting me earlier into the run than I planned.

Merthyr Mawr Warren Nature Reserve is home to the highest dune in Wales (and the second highest in all of Europe), the Big Dipper, a formidable climb that rewards you with panoramic coastal views. Covering 840 acres (or about 340 international rugby pitches) this dune system is one of the most extensive and unique in Wales, constantly shifting and reshaping itself with the brisk coastal winds. Over time, dunes have settled over the grand limestone cliffs, creating a habitat that supports a surprising variety of life: insects, fungi, and hardy plants have all found a way to thrive here, while the reserve also offers grassland, salt marsh, woodland, and beach.[18] In other words, it's varied, it's interesting, and above all, it's a bloody beautiful slice of Welsh landscape.

It's funny – when I mention Merthyr Mawr to other runners, a look of dread washes over their faces. Some confess that they never really noticed the beauty of it because they were being forced to run up that gargantuan sand dune in the name of fitness.

Matt also informs me that it's where Olympic athletes have trained, so I'm starting to think that perhaps this isn't quite the laid-back, scenic 11K run I'd originally expected.

Still. Whatever. It's Friday.

*

The car park is completely empty at 9am on a weekday. Clambering to peer across the sea wall, I get a sweeping view over Newton Beach and today, the tide has pulled back, left its gloss of salt, its undulating lines in the sand where the waves once reached. Pebbles shine, still wet upon the shore. The dunes, soft-backed and golden, watch from the edge as we begin the performance of hamstring stretches, tib raises, and other recommended contortions we're supposed to be doing as runners.

After a few weeks of rushing around between workshops and readings in between my job as a marketing manager, this day off to explore the wilderness is much-needed. Keeping a writing career going alongside a full-time job is often a source of exhaustion for writers; and in the writing world, there's not much time for standing still. Things move fast. New releases push out older ones and there's always that fear that your work will disappear into the void. Yet the contradictory thing is, that we need that time for standing still and making space for ideas. We've got to somehow get comfortable with stepping back for a while, even if it means feeling left behind.

Of course, I could be spending this morning having a deliciously lazy breakfast in bed, but while the weather is being so generous, I'm feeling the pull of the trails. This is happening more often now. The part of me that once obsessed about running is fully back and forever keen to take her trail shoes out to tackle more mud. There are strange, yet welcome things happening with my creativity. The more I'm running, the more I'm writing: not just these chapters, of course, but in the last few weeks I've found myself scribbling sharp-edged, imagistic poems out of nowhere. This is a rarity for me after the release of a poetry collection; usually, the project has sucked the life out of my poetic side and I need to recharge.

But no, I'm surprising myself with new poems that *feel* new – poems that aren't the leftovers from the book I've just written but something entirely different. I've even been scribbling short stories, which is something I haven't done since my MA year at Swansea University 11 years ago. Normally, a sharp little voice of self-doubt will stop me in my tracks after attempting the first paragraph, but the more I run, the quieter that voice is, and the easier the writing feels.

Perhaps it's the confidence boost of having made it up a hill I didn't think I could haul myself up. Perhaps it's the deeper connection with nature and the world around me.

Whatever magic this is, I'll take it. And yes, I'll be milking it for as long as it damn well lasts.

★

I load up my app and immediately take us towards the dunes. Five seconds later, my phone buzzes like an exasperated teacher, telling me I'm already off track, which I think is actually a new personal best in getting lost.

I apologise and redirect us onto Beach Road, passing the pubs and the church and into residential cul-de-sacs. Now, this is where it gets confusing. My app directs me to the walls of houses, then off into dead ends. We decide to ignore it and hop over a wooden stile into a field bristling with gorse and tall grass.

I decide I am not climbing through someone's bathroom window for the sake of following a poorly-mapped route.

After a few minutes of navigating fields bristly with dried shrubbery, the earth beneath our trainers slowly gives way to sand. We pause at a map and study it with hopeful intensity, just in case this will help us understand it. It does not. It's a ribbon of lines with a few arrows pointing in different directions; basically nothing that makes much sense (at least not to me). Still, this is a loop, which means that in theory, we'll end up back where we started. This is good enough for us.

I keep my app fired up just in case we end up so far out we consider getting rescued, but for today, we're going with whatever the hell we feel like.

★

Light pools, then scatters. A flicker through leaves, through the fine mesh of branches that shift in the winter sun. The wind moves, but softly, as if careful not to disturb the foliage. We choose the path that won't trip us up with roots the size of human arms. A woodpecker drills at a trunk, somewhere above our heads. I realise I've never really heard that sound so closely before; I've possibly only ever heard it in cartoons.

The path bends, disappears, and we follow.

This is the longest run Ian has done in quite a while (he is more commonly found wearing Lycra and greasing bike gears) but he's moving in front of me steadily, his breath laboured, but not quite as laboured as my own. Matt, with his short strides, honestly just looks as though he's here to admire the trees and daydream.

He's a big believer in the power of 80/20 running: essentially, the 80/20 rule of running training states that 80% of your weekly training time should be done at an easy effort level, with 20% consisting of harder running.[19] The approach is based on research showing that elite endurance athletes train this way to maximise performance and reduce injury risk. 80/20 training looks like this:

- 80% of runs - These should be done at a low intensity, meaning you should be able to hold a conversation without gasping for breath. This builds aerobic endurance and allows for higher training volume without excessive fatigue.

- 20% of runs - These should be performed at a moderate to high intensity, including tempo runs, intervals, and sprints to improve speed and strength.

The goal is to avoid the "moderate-intensity trap", where runners train too hard on easy days and not hard enough on speed days (yes, I'm guilty). This means it's far easier to keep improving and becoming more efficient without burning out or becoming injured. It's certainly worked for Matt, who's achieving phenomenal times in his fell races, and it's enough to convince me to give this method a go. I've been stuck at the same frustrating pace for what feels like forever, grinding out miles without seeing much in the way of improvement. But, slowly and surely, things are shifting. Week by week, I find it easier to keep my heart rate in check on those easy runs, and – almost without noticing – I'm getting around my usual routes just that little bit faster.

I'll admit, I don't follow it quite so religiously when I'm out on the trails. Trying to maintain a low heart rate while battling steep climbs, uneven terrain, and the occasional bramble bush feels almost impossible at times. But I figure that still counts as hill training (especially when my heart rate monitor spends half the run blinking at me in mild panic).

Hopefully, by the time this book is published, I will be in the Olympics – or, if I'm being realistic, knock a minute or so off my pace.

★

We pull up short, just before wading straight into what can only be described as a swamp of unknown origin. It's mud, but definitely infused with something far more agricultural, given the unmistakable stench and the lazy congregation of cows nearby, watching us dopily with mouths full of grass. We detour, picking our way around the worst of it, hoping not to end up swallowed by something that was inside a cow mere hours ago.

Ahead of us, just beyond a fence, a huge bull stares straight at us, a vast muscled slab of an animal. His coat gleams, rich brown over a frame that's clearly built for power. His skull is thick, heavy, formidable. There is no doubt in my mind that he could plough straight through that fence if the mood took him. He is a beautiful yet terrifying creature. I think I'd like to put him in a poem one day but right now I'm too busy checking my map, praying that we don't have to cross him.

The path we need to follow is the gravel path on the safe side of the fence, much to my relief. The bull keeps his eyes fixed on us as we pass, huffing hot clouds of breath as we begin our pleasing descent down easier roads. A sign informs us we are not so far from Candleston Castle.

Like five-year-olds at Disneyland, we are all excited at the prospect of a castle.

There's a need for deft footwork here. As we gather speed over wobbly rocks and dry earth, I wonder, briefly, if today is the day I finally twist my ankle. This terrain is not unlike the steep, winding path down from Castell Coch, except without the added thrill of a sheer drop to my immediate left. If I fall, well, I'll just end up with a sore ankle and a dusty backside. I'm sure the two boys can reluctantly haul me back to the car like a mud-splattered swamp princess.

We keep going. The path continues to drop.

And drop. And drop some more. A sign had optimistically suggested that Candleston Castle was only half a mile away, but unless my growing paranoia about rolling an ankle is somehow distorting time itself, that distance feels considerably longer.

But hey, at least we're going down and not up.

Eventually, we reach a car park offering a few different paths. There's an information board perched at one end of the car park, so we check it, only to learn that we are already at the castle. We look around, confused. If there was a castle here, surely we couldn't miss a pile of gargantuan rocks and turrets.

Merthyr Mawr

Ian points it out behind a thick copse of trees, so we decide to head over. How exciting. How *romantic*. A secret woodland castle!

Candleston Castle is – yep, you've guessed it – actually a fortified manor. At this point, I am not surprised by this fact; so many of them are. But that doesn't make it any less magical: stone crumbling back on itself in the bright morning light, rooms that have become rubbled ghosts of themselves over centuries, and walls split open to the sky. A tower shrugs itself into ivy, archways leading to blank air. Before I know it, I'm tapping out a note into my trusty Poetry Notes file on my phone:

> *Now, the only things that pass through are wind and ghosts.*
> *And you, standing in the wreckage,*
> *waiting for the dunes to slither down softly,*
> *to answer you back in a headwind of sand.*

I can always count on a good castle (or fortified manor) to inspire me. The only part of this manor still standing with any real conviction is the fourteenth-century tower, once home to the Cantilupes (not melons), a family wealthy enough to build a castle but unfortunately not influential enough to hang onto it for long.

What followed was a centuries-long game of pass-the-parcel with various owners making their mark. The Herberts, who took over in the 1530s, had a go at updating things. Then came Sir John Nicholl, a judge and MP, who slummed it here in the early 1800s while waiting for builders to finish his new and vastly more comfortable mansion, complete with a library big enough to house 30,000 books (which, to be quite honest, is now one of my life goals).

But let's talk about the mystery woman of 1822: a so-called "lady" who decided Candleston was the perfect spot to set up an exclusive sorority. She invited other women to live with her, but only those of, and I quote, "respectable connections".

You go, girl.

By the Twentieth century, the castle had been put to various uses, including a farmhouse, before eventually being left to the elements – though not before the military turned the surrounding dunes into a rifle range. For years, territorial soldiers took potshots out west, their bullets skimming the sand and, occasionally, striking unsuspecting civilians, which is precisely what happened in 1914. Poor Margaret Bishop of Bridgend was out enjoying a walk in the woods when she found herself on the receiving end of a stray bullet to the leg (not quite the tranquil afternoon she had in mind). The culprit was a ricochet, no doubt off a tree, or perhaps off Candleston itself.

It's hard to picture it now, as we trudge up the steps and peer into the shadowy room below: an unsettling little space that, when caught in the harsh glare of a camera flash, looks like the perfect setting for a low-budget horror film. We linger just long enough to poke our heads inside, confirm that no ghosts or axe-wielding maniacs are lurking, and move on. Our heart rates have dropped considerably by the time we've finished posing from the top doing a royal wave.

★

Once we've staggered out of the castle and chosen a direction, there's a brief temptation to tackle The Big Dipper (you know, the second-largest sand dune in Europe). It sounds impressive until you realise it means an obscene amount of uphill trudging in shifting sand, in what's turning out to be a very warm morninng. Matt, ever the optimist, informs me once again that actual Olympians have trained here, which is precisely the moment I decide we are going nowhere near it.

To be honest, I'm already mentally halfway home, curled up in my softest loungewear and clutching a hot mug of coffee.

In fact, let me say this with absolute conviction: one of life's great, underrated pleasures is the post-exertion ache. I love the glow that comes from knowing you've done something difficult and now the universe owes you comfort. There is nothing like that moment where you drag on the ugliest, softest clothes you own, collapse onto a freshly-made bed, and just exist in the warm, blissed-out fog of having done a bloody good run somewhere beautiful. You lie there, marinated in endorphins, with your legs doing that nice achey-twitch thing and your heart ticking gently in your chest.

Sometimes, during these moments, I might flick through a book and sometimes I might scroll through reviews on the route I've just done. Sometimes, I'll just lie back, close my eyes, and engage in the highest form of meditation known to humankind: the considered fantasy of what kind of pizza I want to order later. Whether I end up choosing wild mushroom or pepperoni or some chaotic Frankenstein hybrid with hot honey and burrata is irrelevant (in fact, it's usually margherita because I'm dull). But the point is, I'll have bloody earned it.

Waving goodbye to the Big Dipper, we bounce through some woodland that feels slightly like Jurassic Park and end up facing a wide sand dune, churned by footfall and stunningly gold in the sunshine. I could almost trick myself into believing I was in Lanzarote were it not for the blare of very Welsh accents shouting after their dogs.

This stretch of sand means uphill progress is inevitably slow.

And just when we think we're over the worst of it, we're onto thin ribbons of the stuff, churning below our heels. From this dry scrubland, we can see the distant sea winking at us, little sparks of light catching the waves. We're on the home stretch, but as my glutes and quads burn through each heavy step, my car might as well be on the other side of the planet.

The good thing is that my legs are getting stronger after weeks of cresting hills and spending my weekday mornings pulling barbells. My running bottoms are getting tight around the thighs which, ten years ago, would have felt somewhat devastating to me.

Not anymore. I'm enjoying seeing the thick quad muscle beginning to swell above my knee and embracing a stronger self that's more creative, more chilled, and much, much stronger. This hasn't been an automatic shift in perspective, but today, I realise, I'm feeling a little more positive about myself.

It wasn't always this way. If you'd told university-aged me that one day I'd be voluntarily spending two mornings a week in a private gym, deadlifting, hip-thrusting, and, dare I say it, doing pretty bloody well at Nordic curls, I would have laughed in your face (assuming I had the energy). I was deep in the trenches of an eating disorder then, waging war on my own body, hell-bent on whittling myself down to the smallest version possible. I was still dealing with the fallout of years of school bullying, frustrated with my diabetes, and struggling against the suffocating expectation that women should take up less space: physically, socially, existentially.

Weightlifting for women? The old me would have scoffed: *no thanks*. It simply wasn't on the radar. Lifting was for men, the sort who could mainline protein powder and sprout biceps overnight. Meanwhile, women were conditioned to fear muscle like it was some kind of disease. *Stay small. Look pretty. Don't make noise.* This was simply a lifelong script we didn't question, learned from magazine covers, fashion runways, and pop culture at large.

But things are changing. The #StrongNotSkinny and #WomenWhoLift hashtags show how weightlifting for women has exploded in popularity. Walters and Heffernan's (2020) qualitative study examined the impact of resistance training on positive body image in women aged 35–50 years. The findings reported that resistance training allowed participants to develop greater appreciation and acceptance of their bodies, and they became less fixated on weight and size, instead focusing on their physical strength and power. Despite continuing to harbour negative feelings about certain body parts, the participants expressed positive feelings and appreciation toward their body's physical abilities.[20]

Merthyr Mawr

It doesn't come as a surprise when I think about this. When you're deadlifting more than your own body weight, you start to see yourself differently – not as a fragile thing to be preserved, but as a powerful, capable force to be reckoned with.

For years, we were told that exercise was a punishment. It was merely a means of repentance for the crime of eating. It was about shrinking, about earning our place in the world by taking up less of it. But strength training rewrites the script somewhat. It is not about whittling yourself down to a more palatable version. It is about building. It's about seeing what your body can do and how much it can lift.

This isn't just hopeful rhetoric; it's backed by research. The study by Walters and Heffernan looked at women aged 35 to 50 who took up resistance training, and the findings were quietly radical. These women, conditioned for decades to worry about weight and size, found themselves thinking less about measurements and more about power. Their legs could lift. Their arms could press. Their backs could carry. They still had small complaints about a 'problem' body part here and there (after all, self-perception, like muscle, is not built overnight) but they spoke about themselves with something astonishing: *appreciation*.

It turns out that lifting heavy things and putting them back down again does something quite brilliant to your brain. It shifts the focus from appearance to action. Instead of spending hours picking themselves apart in the mirror, these women were standing taller and feeling stronger. And perhaps that's what's most important: strength training doesn't just help you accept your body.

It makes you *proud* of it.

And as these strong thighs churn through the difficult sand dunes ahead, I think I finally get it.

★

We soon reach the recognisable stretch of field we encountered at the start, but I must have been looking too closely because

I didn't notice the willow branch flinging itself straight at my eye.

I try, with some difficulty, not to make a spectacle of myself in front of the others. This mostly involves a lot of swearing and some aggressive rubbing at my eyelid, which is now bleeding. I ask Ian to check it, while trying not to cry.

He says I will live.

By the time we hit the road again, legs deliciously heavy, the world feels brighter. The sun's climbed higher. The town is waking up. Daffodils flare along the verge like little yellow candles.

Someone mentions breakfast, which is an appealing prospect. But first, we chug water at the car in massive gulps, toss muddy shoes into the boot, and stand there for a moment watching the tide throw itself up to the shore. I am still rubbing my sore eye.

Merthyr Mawr, you've been gorgeous and wild. Let's do this again sometime.

(I'll bring protective goggles.)

Salmon Leaps

Location
Salmon Leaps and Caerau Hill Fort, Dinas Powys
ST 15248 71287

Distance
12K

Parking
Street parking in Dinas Powys.

Facilities
The Cross Keys pub in Dinas Powys is a beautiful place to rehydrate and refuel at the end, especially outside on a balmy sunny afternoon.

Tips
You can miss the hill fort and just do Salmon Leaps if you want to make it a little shorter (many people skip this bit). The climb up to Caerau Hill Fort isn't the prettiest, but if you like old, dilapidated churches, you'll probably like the gothic vibes once you get to the top.

Salmon Leaps

I'll be honest here: I didn't actually pick this route for any profound reason. I didn't research it deeply or spend time looking at the elevation profile or nearby facilities.

I just really liked the name.

Dinas Powys village itself is in full bloom on this warm April day, a riot of wildflowers, frothing cherry blossoms and charming old stone buildings. I could almost believe that I hadn't been dragging along the stretch of M4 motorway for the past hour; the village is a little world contained in itself. It's gorgeous, in a way that could fool me into thinking I was driving through the set of Emmerdale or maybe Midsomer Murders.

There are no murderers about, but there are a lot of runners zipping into Casehill Woods, faces slick with sweat and fists curled at their sides (presumably because they are exercising and not because they are being chased by psychopaths).

I wince as I pull myself up and out of the car, having hurt both knees doing speed work in the week *and* then somehow managing to pull my glute doing a bike ride with far too many uphill stretches. At this rate, by the end of this book I'll be a soft pile of bones on the living room carpet, dictating my last words to Siri, which will probably be something about orthopaedic cushions.

★

This run offers a beautiful slice of ancient woodland with Cwm George being the first place I encounter, home to the kestrel and rare hazel dormouse. It's among the oldest broadleaved forests in the Vale of Glamorgan, with pale beeches, small-leaved limes, and hazels tucked away in the undergrowth. There are rowan trees too, stripped of their blinking autumnal berries. I've started to develop a new, low-level obsession with trees. I talk to them sometimes, even if it's just in my head. I thank them when they catch my fall or provide a spot of shade when I stop to pee, squatting like a terrified meerkat, eyes darting for signs of passing dog walkers.

Sometimes, poems are the closest I can get to conversation:

Tell it to the trees
to the branches cupped in your open palm
blooming to sudden angles, pale as candles
melting down, a swell of leaves unlatching
in the last of the yellow afternoon
when the sun is a shrinking balloon
untethered from your grasp, when the clouds
unclasp and the dark earth steams with drizzle.[21]

There is no sign of any such drizzle today. Part of me wonders if this sudden, unseasonal brightness is a trick. Perhaps it's merely a prelude to one of those damp, midge-infested summers where the only barbecues are the ones you watch from the window, angrily munching a tub of coleslaw. Maybe we're burning through our quota of good days too early and summer will be torrential. Whatever the reason, I'm making the most of it, because it's so much easier to fall in love with each location when it's not pissing down.

The cycles of these seasons stand for the cycles I've learned to understand in the creative process. The roots of these trees spread far beneath the soil, anchoring to the earth and pulling in the essential nutrients that have kept them growing for hundreds of years. This hidden work has more recently become a metaphor for the hidden work of the creative process: the stages of preparation and incubation as identified by Graham Wallas in his study of creativity, *The Art of Thought*

(1926). Wallas described these early stages as the time when a person is quietly gathering information, reflecting and letting the mind quietly work on the problem at hand. In this state, it may look like nothing is happening externally, but underneath the mind is connecting, synthesising and rooting itself in creative ideas.

This quiet period is essential for creativity. Without taking time to lay these roots, I have no hope of creative work growing. "This then," I think, slapping my heels against the muddy tracks, "is the permission I need to let go." It's my sign to keep running and stop struggling with trying to find the next thunderbolt of creative brilliance.

*

There's a gentle rush of water beside me and I cross a little wooden bridge, emerging through a path onto a golf course. Why must every run come with a golf course lately?

I hug the perimeter of the field, panicking slightly at the signs that tell me to beware of golf balls that could potentially whistle directly onto my skull. Fortunately, I'm out of it quickly and onto a road thick with the sound and noise of farm life: tractors roar behind hedgerows and a pony drags its chin across a fencepost, tending to an itch that apparently won't disappear. It's uphill from here so I power on, pausing only to admire the glassy surface of the river beyond the fence. We'll get more acquainted with this beautiful river later, but for now, I'm already satisfied with the variety this run is offering me before I've even ticked off my first couple of kilometres.

*

The farm roads along Michaelston-le-Pit are long and they smell, to put it politely, pretty potent. To my right, cows lurch about lazily in the field, occasionally flicking their tails at flies and ignoring the roaring tractor in the next field over, which is enthusiastically spreading whatever those cows probably passed through their digestive tracts before breakfast.

My knee is in agony. It's my own fault, of course. I should have taken the advice from my physio app and stayed home to raise my hips on a bouncy exercise ball or perfect my tib raises. But no, here I am, strapped from ankle to knee, pounding the hard gravel beneath me, trying to make the most of a stunningly bright Saturday morning because I'm stubborn and because I'm very aware of the impending book deadline.

I stop, several times. My insulin pump trembles from somewhere in the depths of my sports bra.

My body really seems to be against me today. Heat speeds everything up: metabolism, insulin absorption, heart rate, panic. What starts as a pleasant April morning can become a sweat-soaked hypo waiting to happen. The problem is, I don't want running to become something I only do when all the variables are perfect. I don't want to wait for a time when my blood sugar is steady, when the weather's kind, or when I'm injury-free and full of energy. Because if I waited for that, I'd barely leave the house.

It's Fruit Pastilles today, already sticky and flat. The first one is orange. I check underneath and it's another orange one.

This annoys me even more.

I pass a few early-morning dog walkers with very well-behaved collies and labradors trotting alongside obediently. We greet each other, because this is what people do before 11am, especially in charming Welsh villages.

*

I'm nearing the climb to Caerau Hill Fort. I'm surprised to be spat out onto a road with cars flying over the bypass above. Beside me, chain-link fences give the place a worn, industrial feel, a world away from that ancient woodland I'd zipped through at the start.

My app informs me I'm to clamber over a forlorn-looking

fence surrounded by empty Lucozade bottles and dog poo bags, which doesn't feel very noble for a hill fort. I clamber anyway, performing a graceless little tumble like a wardrobe being flung down a flight of stairs. Gymnastics were never my strong point.

I'll admit that I have to walk some of this as the gradient is brutal on my knees. The ascent isn't the prettiest; I feel like I've wandered into an uphill version of 'Smoker's Lane'. This was the unavoidable path into school where a line of rucksacks would bob through its wrought-iron jaws, beneath the hard stare of teens chomping on spearmint Wrigley's and lighting up smuggled Pall Malls.

This time, there's no risk of getting spat on, which is nice.

I stop to pee behind a tree. I've needed to go since I left my car, but I'd been put off by all the parents swinging toddlers in their hands and throwing tennis balls for dogs. Up here, I can't ruin anyone's day with the sight of me squatting down ungracefully because there's no one else about. Even on the reviews for this trail, many people skip this climb.

I'm too curious to skip it and besides, a hill fort sounds pretty important.

I sort myself out (thank you trees, for your generous abundance of leaves) and continue up the path on a slight left until I reach the crest of the hill. In front of me, a church stands as though placed there specifically for a Netflix horror film: the roof long gone, the windows hollowed out, and the gravestones leaning as if I've stumbled upon them mid-conversation. A crisp packet skitters along the foot of a wall, catching the light in a moment of strange, accidental grace.

This is St Mary's Church, which although restored in the early 1960s, was once again deconsecrated in 1973 and has subsequently fallen into ruin due to vandalism.[22] Despite its slow descent into disrepair, I think there's something oddly beautiful about these ruins, starkly contrasting against the bright April sky.

Built between 1254 and 1291 in the Early English style, on

land once occupied by a Roman fort, it may not have been the first church on this site. Its early years are sparsely recorded, but we know that in 1535 the church tithes were paid to the Prebendary of Llandaff Cathedral. The Reformation brought destruction: murals were whitewashed, the rood loft torn out, ornaments sold.

The church changed hands with each monarch's whim: Catholic under Mary I, Protestant again under Elizabeth I. A skeleton and seventeenth-century buttons were once found near the ancient yew tree, believed to be over 2,000 years old before it was destroyed by fire in 1937. These items were thought to be from a grave, but this grave has not been found and no grave dates before the eighteenth century.

After its closure in 1957, St Mary's suffered years of neglect and vandalism. Windows were bricked up, the roof removed, and its ancient bell stolen. Yet in the 1960s, under the care of Reverend Victor Jones and volunteers, the church was slowly restored. It was rehallowed in 1961, briefly returning to life – holding services, weddings, and funerals – before crumbling into the state of disrepair in front of me today.

Since 1999, a small group has gathered under the name Friends of St Mary's Church, Caerau. Quietly, steadily, they have worked to protect what remains.

Old buildings, especially those that once held communities such as churches, schools, and halls, seem to absorb something of the people who passed through them. You don't have to believe in ghosts to feel it. Even when crumbling, I think they offer a kind of continuity.

I'm now wondering where this fort is. I bounce past the church and emerge onto a flat, circular patch of grass that gives a stunning view over the western suburbs of Caerau and Ely in Cardiff.

I don't know why, but when I read "Iron Age hill fort" I was expecting to find something grand, teeming with warriors even though it is 2025 and people do not need to have fights on these hills anymore.

I circle there for a while before realising this is the hill fort.

CAER Heritage Project gives me a bit of enlightenment on this mysterious place, which is apparently "the largest Iron Age hillfort in south Glamorgan, but until recently had been almost entirely overlooked by archaeologists. The ramparts of the hillfort are hidden beneath woodland, a fact that means many people, even those living in the shadow of the great monument, don't even realise it is there."[23]

I later discover that I'm standing upon a wealth of buried history, and that excavations by the CAER Heritage Project have revealed that the hillfort was densely occupied, its slopes once dotted with Iron Age roundhouses dating back to around 600 BC. The site remained active well into the Roman period and beyond, enduring and adapting with the centuries. Some historians think it may have once been a court of the kings of Glamorgan, nestled here in what was once the power centre of early medieval Wales. Spears have been found. Swords too. It's clear this was a place worth defending.

I sit for a moment, looking down over the Western side of the Welsh capital and pushing not-very-Iron-Age Fruit Pastilles into my mouth with a shaking hand until my legs feel stable enough to tackle the descent back down.

I'm glad I came up here. It feels like I've stumbled upon a secret.

★

Before long, I'm back on the farm path, retracing my steps past the field where the pony, now having finished its vigorous chin-scratch on the fence post, is standing motionless with a mouthful of grass, eyeing me warily like I might be back to sell something.

There's a slight elevation gain here as the path disappears into woodland, the light dimming as if someone's drawn a sheer curtain over the day. The trees gather closer, their branches interlacing overhead. This is Coed Penllwynog, which I follow down towards Cadoxton River.

Running down this path is like splitting an invisible sea straight through the forest; inky bluebells bloom from the undergrowth, swelling from shadow as if nudged into life by my passing. Overhead, butterflies swing towards the light as I follow its gentle loop. Both bluebell and butterfly feel like signposts of something fleeting – delicate, seasonal markers that arrive quietly and vanish just as fast. They're here now, fluttering at the edges of the path, nodding gently in the breeze, but they won't be for long. The heat will come. The blossoms will drop. Other things will bloom and then fall.

> *The bluebells are gossiping again.*
> *A butterfly, dressed for some tiny,*
> *impossible party, vanishes*
> *into a shaft of light*
> *then peels away.*

The most we can do is to capture these fleeting moments before the seasons change again. For some people it's photographs. For me, it's usually poetry.

The closer I get to the stream in Winstone Brook, the more the terrain begins to unravel beneath me. The path narrows and kinks, tree roots knuckle up through the mud, and suddenly I'm clambering, occasionally ducking under low branches, sidestepping fallen trunks, arms outstretched for balance.

It's clumsy, but I love it. I feel like some sort of Welsh Indiana Jones, if Indiana Jones wore striped, pink leggings and stopped every ten minutes to admire a nice leaf or check their insulin pump.

The brook gurgles just out of sight, getting louder. At about 8km long, it's actually one of Wales's shortest rivers, despite the ache in my legs. Here, deep in the woodland, the water is brown and murky, hissing softly over the mud as I navigate my way alongside it. So far, it's fairly unremarkable; no different to the ruddy waters I've passed on routes through the woods in Gower (usually while trying to swat horseflies off my face, flailing and screaming like a terrified monkey).

Salmon Leaps

This river is about to surprise me. There's a reason this route was once featured in an article by *The Times*, detailing '20 of the UK's most beautiful woodlands for winter walks'.

I emerge onto Salmon Leaps. The name holds a hopeful promise of silvery flashes rising through the current, of motion against gravity, of something muscling ferociously upstream. But in truth, salmon sightings are rare here now. The weirs simply cascade into blankness, the water folding into steady rhythm. The leapers, however, have mostly moved on or vanished.

Or, perhaps, they simply refuse to perform for passers-by on cue.

A group of ramblers has paused ahead of me, pointing at something in the middle of the water. Beside them, a photographer is crouched into position, oblivious to their chatter and determined to capture the perfect shot.

I jog ahead for a few metres before I see it for myself: a heron, raising its neck into a practised stretch as though pausing for breath. I realise this is the first time I've really seen a heron this close in the wild. The wind lifts a few feathers from its back and puts them down again. It stares into the water like it's trying to remember a pin number.

The photographer ahead shifts on the bank and the shutter clicks: once, twice, a stutter of wings caught in stasis. The foam slides past its ankles. I watch a leaf bounce off its leg. It doesn't move. For something so graceful and otherworldly, there's something oddly domestic about it.

I stay here for a while, watching it. My insulin pump, for once, lets me do this undisturbed without yelping for more glucose. In the field above me, a creamy-coloured horse drags its heft along the grass, its belly heavy with foal.

My head tells me I should write something, but I don't. Sometimes I just need to be fully present.

If it wants to be written, it'll come back later, persistently, like an angry horsefly.

★

I'm onto the final stretch and boy, do my knees know it. I stop several times to hitch up the knee support and wriggle my ankles. I perform several tib raises against the sturdy trunk of a beech tree. I glance down at my map and see that I'm coming up to Dinas Powys Castle and begin wondering whether it's a castle at all or just another manor in disguise.

Good news: it is indeed a castle. Although I can barely see it (I could clamber up the muddy banks towards it but honestly neither me not my knees can be bothered), I do crane my neck to at least get a glimpse of its walls. It's pretty ruined.

What remains today is just a shell: the curtain wall, crumbling in parts, thick with lichen and the stump of a keep, its stone softened into rubble, but still square-shouldered enough to hint that it used to be something far grander. The site is older than it appears. Originally fortified in the early Christian period, between the fifth and sixth centuries, it evolved over time. A wooden ringwork was replaced with stone, the defences were rebuilt and extended as the landscape changed hands. Postholes and fragments of revetment hint at early palisades and fighting platforms, while traces of an entrance and timber gate suggest a more watchful past.

The most interesting thing to note about this castle is that its remains can be traced back to Iron Age, Roman, Dark Age, Saxon and Norman fortifications.

Maybe it's the castle that's distracted me or maybe it's just the fact that I cannot work out which way is left and which way is right, but I end up doing some confused loops around the final part of Casehill Woods, trying to find my way back to the little village (and a nice little cold drink).

I'm already dreading the comments on my Strava when these little loops become apparent: "Were you lost again, Nat?" Hopefully some nice pictures of herons will distract them from the wildly looping GPS doodles.

These woods are clearly a popular running destination, as several similarly sweaty runners wave in greeting and disappear into the trees. I think, if I lived in this lovely little

Salmon Leaps

village, I would absolutely make this my main running route, too. I'd lace up and run this route again and again, until even the muddled loops began to feel like home.

*

Finally, I'm done. My watch tells me I've done over 13K now, so I can justify the walk back up the pavement towards the village. I know exactly where I'm going to stop: The Cross Keys, which sits just off from the roundabout into the village, with its quaint little beer garden beneath baskets of cheerful flowers.

I order a water and an icy Pepsi Max and stretch out on the edge of shade, letting the quiet of the village settle around me. There's birdsong, the clink of cutlery, and someone's dog snoozing under a table nearby. The air smells faintly of cut grass and cheese-and-onion crisps.

I think this was one of my favourite routes, and perhaps, one I'm most proud of because I did it alone on a day when my body was against me. My knees ached. My blood sugar dipped, then dipped again. I had no real plan, no one to follow, nothing but a tiny, battery-anxious GPS map glowing in the palm of my hand.

And yes, I pissed in the woods. Yes, I ate almost an entire packet of Fruit Pastilles to get through the relentless hypos. And yes, I got a little lost. And already, I can't wait to tell people about it; not just the run, but the castle, the heron, the bluebells spilling into shadow, and the way the trees closed around me and then opened again like they were taking a breath. With so much history, so many shifting landscapes, and a rare pocket of stillness just beyond the reach of the city, I think for me, it was worth doing this route in its entirety.

The annoying thing is, every time I mention this route to someone, it's not a secret at all. They already know.

It's a good thing it's one you can return to, over and over again.

Cefn Bryn

Location
Cefn Bryn, Ryers Down, Landimore and Oldwalls
SS 49083 90028

Distance
Approx 14K

Parking
Free parking at the top of Cefn Bryn (get there early in warmer months).

Facilities
Toilets, food and drinks at the King Arthur pub just down the road.

Tips
Time your run so you catch the sunset. Trust me, you'll be rewarded with a riot of bronze light slathered over dramatic hills. It's bloody lush.

Cefn Bryn

If you're planning on doing some Gower visits, I think it's important to highlight the side of Gower that is so often ignored: North Gower. It happens to be closest to home for me, which does make it convenient, but that's not why it's earned a place in this book. It's got variety. It's got elevation. It's got views that take your breath away (or maybe that's just the elevation).

My decision to run that particular trail today comes to me in a moment of pure, undiluted boredom. It's a gloriously sunny Monday afternoon after an early finish in work, and I'm languishing in that strange existential void between lunch and dinner, sitting at my desk in loungewear, spooning yogurt into my mouth (protein after that day's lifting session, I tell myself, and not just mindless snacking). I toy briefly with the idea of setting my Sims on fire again, but I've done that three times over the weekend already and the novelty of digital arson has worn thin.

As the sun spreads over the freshly-cut lawn and the gulls crash-land onto the neighbour's roof, I realise I just really want to be outside. I've had enough of shimmering screens for one day.

I tug my garish purple running tights on and decide I'll go somewhere away from the M4 this evening. I don't want slip roads. I don't want the grim orchestra of traffic. I want space. I want the countryside. I want the sour, unmistakable tang of freshly manured farmland mingling with the scent of gorse. I want the most dramatic views this side of Gower can offer me.

So I get in the car and point it towards Cefn Bryn – what's

known as 'the backbone of Gower', a lumpy, brooding ridgeline that manages to be both bleak and beautiful at once.
Perfect for a poet.

★

Parking is easy in late March. My only company is a man with a motorbike, snapping pictures of the view, and a woman in running gear looking unfazed by having charged up the hill without stopping. I would like that sort of energy. I've had an exhausting day looking at Google Analytics and twirling on my chair, which has really taken it out of me.

I fill my sports bra with packets of Jelly Babies and plunge a bag of Skittles into my pocket (elite hypo treatments). I hit my Garmin and set off, straight in front of the car park and over pleasingly bouncy grass. I pop my headphones on and press play, letting sweeping post-rock tingle in my ears.

I tell myself I'll be back well before dinner.

★

Within a few short steps, the first real landmark appears: King Arthur's Stone. Or to give it its proper title, *Maen Ceti*, which I think is rather beautiful to say (as so many Welsh names are).

King Arthur's Stone squats on Cefn Bryn as if dropped there by a passing giant who forgot his shopping. If local lore is to be believed, then King Arthur himself hurled the stone from Carmarthenshire after removing a stone from his shoe (for some reason, I'm imagining him shopping in Trostre retail park and shaking his shoe outside River Island). Touched by King Arthur's hand, the stone then grew in size, to this great lump of rock I have here in front of me today.

The landmark is actually a Neolithic burial tomb dating back to around 2500 BCE.[24] The capstone weighs approximately 25 tonnes, and some say a local miller took a hammer to it, quite fancying a new millstone for himself, only to realise that several tonnes of prehistoric rock are not easily wheeled down a country lane.

Others prefer a more cinematic explanation in the form of a bolt of lightning, thrown by the hands of Gods, splitting the rock in a fit of impressive pyrotechnics. And others believe perhaps it was cleaved in two by St. David himself, wielding a sword in a rage against pagan Druid rituals.

The far less glamorous (and more likely) explanation is the one that it's simply the work of winter frost. Water finds a crack, freezes, expands, and eventually, the capstone just kind of pops. So, there were probably no pebbles in shoes and no magic touch. It's just basic physics ruining everyone's fun and poetic inspiration.

Had any poor recent dating experiences lately? Well, I have another bit of interesting folklore for you. At some point in the past, this ancient tomb was also a kind of supernatural Tinder, offering young women a chance to test the faithfulness of their lovers using a combination of barley, honey, and sorcery.

The woman in question would bake little cakes from barley meal and honey, dip them in milk (is there anything more alluring than soggy carbohydrates?), and place them gently upon the cold, mossy surface of Arthur's Stone.[25] She would then crawl around the monument three times and if, upon the final lap, her beloved miraculously appeared, he was deemed loyal and worth keeping. If not, he was dumped straight into the emotional recycling bin.

Naturally, this sounds less like a legitimate test of romantic fidelity and more like the result of a few too many meads. But I still think it's an interesting slice of folklore; it's so incredibly human in its wishful logic, yet pretty unbothered by the practical details. For example, how was the lover supposed to know he (or she) was meant to appear in the first place?

Still, there's something almost moving about romantic drama, insecurity, and cake coming together on an ancient burial mound.

Even if the lover in question, the poor sod, never stood a chance.

*

Look east from the stone and the whole of Loughor Estuary opens out before you, all silver mudflats and winding rivers. I can see across the water to the place where I first fell in love with running.

Here I am, eighteen years later, still addicted to the high. My knee is sore and strapped up; but physiotherapists all know the stubbornness of a dedicated runner. I know enough of my fellow runners who have tape strapped to every conceivable bit of flesh on their legs or have fully dosed up on ibuprofen, or maybe spent hundreds on massage guns and the hands of overenthusiastic chiropractors. I've got what I suspect is the start of an old IT band issue (told you I'd whinge about injuries), but I will rest tomorrow.

I can't promise, though.

Even at this obscure time of day, people are beginning to gather around King Arthur's Stone, phones poised, hinting at me to shove off out of the way. I stubbornly oblige (not before I've snapped a photo for my own camera reel first) and send the photo to Ian to proudly prove I'm not lost, even though I've only moved a few metres away from the car park.

Everyone I know and love has little faith in my navigation and honestly, I have no idea why.

*

Only a little way ahead of King Arthur's Stone is the Cefn Bryn Great Cairn, which looks a bit like something from a post-apocalyptic film. The rocks are stacked, here and there, to create an odd, almost alien little piece of natural art. It catches my attention more than *Maen Ceti* does, simply because of the neatness of these stacks; of how people have just left them there, piled curiously, almost asking to be toppled.

I do not topple them. Mainly because I've just noticed that my feet have started sinking through bracken.

Next thing I know, my shoes have disappeared.

It's deceptive, this part of Cefn Bryn. What looks like firm, dried grass will give way to cold, muddy water, which is great if you want to startle yourself awake but not so great if you have no change of shoes in your car.

Obviously, I have no change of shoes in my car.

*

I'm going in a strange curve along this hill, down and then up, and then up some more. By the time I reach the top, I'm greeted with hazy views of Gower, flashes of butter-yellow gorse flowers and, finally, stable ground. Technically, when I'm running in the evening I've got more fuel in the tank than those bleak pre-breakfast shuffles, when my body is simply running on caffeine and mild anger at being made to exert itself so early. But this fuel comes at a price: the weight of the day. It's not that I'm stressed with work or home or anything else. Work's fine, nothing has caught fire at home and the dog hasn't been sick on anything that I'm aware of so far today. I just feel like my brain is *full* and buzzing. It's less a mood than a low-grade hum. If I had to describe it more clearly to you, then it's the mental equivalent of leaving your phone on vibrate on top of a glass table.

Maybe you can relate to this, too. Maybe this is also one of the reasons why you run.

Sometimes, this almost-itchy feeling of anxious energy gives way to bursts of creativity, which would be incredibly convenient given the deadlines I have looming for this week. So, when I take this feeling out on the roads, it often goes one of two ways:

1) I get back from the run transformed. I sit down, open the laptop, and pour out words like I've just channelled John Keats via Strava.

2) I get back grumpier than I left. My body's tired, my legs ache, and the idea of sitting in front of a glowing screen trying to be insightful makes me want to throw my laptop into the nearest body of water and become a shepherd.

On the road, my runs are full-blown mental escapes; a playlist, a podcast and a full-on rant in motion, all contained safely inside my head. I solve things. I rehearse arguments I'll never have. I rewrite emails in my head that I'll never send. I like to think of it as internal theatre, performed at pace.

On the trail, however, all of that melts away. There's no room for cerebral drama when you're concentrating on not face-planting into a pile of cow manure. The terrain needs your full focus and so your body becomes the main event. It's not escapism so much as total presence. It's also remarkably healing, in a way that doesn't require a yoga mat or someone whispering tender affirmations to be gentle with your body over whale noises and using words like 'nourish' (which reminds me, I really ought to drag myself back to yoga class).

Over time, I've learned that my road runs are for escaping into my head. My trail runs are for getting present in my body.

Both have their place.

*

This green expanse of hilltop stretches on for a while, somewhat epic once the *Lord of the Rings* soundtrack pops onto my Spotify and a horse emerges from behind a hedge, as though it's just sniffed out a stray hobbit.

I descend steeply, past charming farmhouses and velvety fields, bobbled with sheep. The skies sweep with crows and, occasionally, a broad-winged buzzard. Whenever I see a new

Cefn Bryn

bird, I can't wait to bore everyone by telling them with all the enthusiasm of a toddler who's just discovered Play-Doh. Only last week I bombarded the family Whatsapp group with photos of a sparrowhawk perched on my fence. I was breathless as I crouched in the conservatory, snapping the photos, not caring that I was in too-small Tom and Jerry pyjamas. As I push on, there are more birds that get me excited: pheasants, with their fabulous, crayon-bright plumes, streaking over the meadows in a blur of browns, reds, and bluebottle-greens.

By now I've corrected a wrong turn not once, not twice, but three times. Why doesn't the arrow on my app point the right bloody way? Either these Strava routes are more complicated than they need to be or my internal compass is completely out of order (it's probably the latter).

This is *definitely* the right stile. It's just that I'm not entirely alone (nor entirely comfortable) in this next field. It's here that I learn a hard, sheep-related lesson which I will share in confidence with you, so that you do not make the same mistake. You know, I'd always believed sheep were the most docile of animals. I pass them often on my walks around Llanrhidian Marsh; occasionally, I'll get a stomp of the foot and a long, slightly demonic stare, but mostly they just amble off the path and do normal, nice, sheep things.

Not these sheep.

I drop over the stile and into the field, admiring their sweet little faces and fantastic puffs of wool. I drop to a walk so as not to startle them.

They start grouping together, walking closer to me. At first, I think this is cute They're curious. They're unfazed. A few steps later, they're picking up the pace.

Feeling a bit unsettled, I pick my pace up too.

They move towards me faster. I now decide it's time to sprint.

Glancing back over my shoulder, I see that the sheep have started bloody running too.

I charge through sheep manure, heels flicking it all up my

back in thick, earthy globs. My heart rate spikes to 175 on my watch (I'm on for a PB on Strava, I think) and I leg it, covered in sheep poo, for the stile at the opposite end of the field until I finally clamber over, gasping and halfway to a panic attack.

Oh, God, the *adrenaline*.

I lean against the safe side of the fence, breathless, vowing never to be fooled by these sweet-faced little puffs of wool again. If it's lambing season and they want to ram you, they will, like fast and aggressive cardigans.

Right now, I am officially the worst I have ever smelled. I can't wait to give Ian a hug later.

★

It takes me a while to get my breath back and work out where I am. I recognise the road to Fairyhill (very extravagant, very beautiful, very expensive wedding venue), then realise my map is telling me to bound off somewhere between the hedges opposite.

I follow the path all the way to the top of Ryer's Down, which is steeper and a little longer than I'd anticipated. There are sheep up here, too. These ones, mercifully, don't seem interested in forming a violent mob. They give me the occasional glance and return to their chewing.

The terrain gets more and more challenging as I move upwards.

By now, I can really *feel* how knackered I am from the week. Not just physically. Creatively. Professionally. Emotionally. I've spent the past few days in that special purgatory reserved for people who voluntarily write things and then ask other people to like them. The rejections have come thick and fast. Emails that begin kindly and end with variations of "not quite right for us", or, "we loved your voice and you made the shortlist, but..." or, more simply, "unfortunately you were not successful".

It doesn't matter that I was on the shortlist or that it wasn't quite the right time or the right place. I'd say I've built a thick skin to rejection. But some weeks, it's one rejection after another. And no matter how many times you go through it, how much perspective you have, how many times you tell yourself it's not personal, there are times when the hurt and self-doubt will find a way in when you least expect it. Rejection chips away at something quiet inside you – not just your work, but your sense of worth. You start to wonder if maybe the stories you have to tell aren't needed. Or worse: that they are, but not from you.

But still, we do it. We keep writing.

Because the only thing worse than rejection is to stop writing altogether.

*

I can feel a familiar tingling and weakness in my legs that tells me my blood sugars are plunging. My head feels a little as though I'm running through a dream, though I have to keep some of my wits about me as the deeply-turned mud has dried in the sun and now threatens to trip me up with one wrong step.

I slow down and pour a small population of Jelly Babies into my mouth.

I stand there chewing like my woolly companions, watching the wind move across the grass, and thinking, for the first time today, that maybe I'll be okay. My lungs are full and heaving. My hair is a wild mess. My eyes, I've only just noticed, are wet, and not just because it's windy. It's rare that a run can give me an emotional purge, but when it does, it feels raw. I'm here and I'm doing this hard thing, while my body is struggling against me. Most importantly, I have no signal to check for another rejection in my email app. It's just me, some bored sheep, and a patchwork of perfectly green fields in the distance.

Running doesn't erase the rejections, or the ache, or the feeling that you might be shouting into a void, but it does remind you that you can still move forward. That your body, for all its protests, can keep going. That your brain, cluttered and buzzing as it may be, can find its way to calmness if you let it.

There's resilience in strapping on your shoes and running anyway. And there's resilience in sending out the pitch, the story, the idea, again. Not because you're guaranteed success, but because not trying feels worse. There are few runs I regret, just the same as there are few writing sessions I regret. It all counts. It's all progress.

I stumble and my ankle catches awkwardly. An orange Jelly Baby flies out of my hand and into the mud.

And because I want to think more positively about things, I tell myself that at least it wasn't a red one.

★

Descending Ryer's Down is difficult when you're navigationally-challenged. What starts as a vaguely defined footpath quickly devolves into a web of thick bramble. I am snared by gorse, scratched like I've fought a furious raccoon, and as I glance down, I clock a twig of hawthorn poking out of my bra. There are leaves in my hair.

After ten minutes of finding nothing but blocked paths, I consider sliding down to the nearest farmhouse and ringing Ian to pick me up, dishevelled, from a stranger's garden.

Fortunately, I am too stubborn and proud for that, so after a few confused loops, I finally manage to push down through the woodlands and onto the road to Landimore.

I've never ventured into this part of Gower before. The roads are eerily empty. A hulking purple bus, devoid of its driver, is parked at the side of the road. Were it not for the faint sounds of bleating in the distance and the warm, syrupy wash of gold evening light, I'd be half-convinced the world had ended while I was being mauled by gorse on the hill.

There's a fair bit of road running ahead before I'm back on farmland. The road is narrow, the hedges are high, and every blind corner brings the possibility of a juddering tractor appearing out of nowhere. I warily jog past sheep and their tiny, delightful lambs. Despite myself, I can't help but admire their little wobbly legs, ears too big for their heads, and faces filled with innocent bewilderment. It's like jogging through a Disney film and I'm Snow White in Lycra.

But I'm not fooled. I look straight into the eyes of an adult sheep, notice its stomping foot, and keep my speed up.

The sun is beginning its descent, dissolving into a scorched orange above the treetops. As I dip through patches of woodland, fronds open out around me in the darkness, emanating sweetness. I recognise the unmistakable smell: wild garlic, with its deep, sweet, earthy pungency that's somehow both fragrant and feral. Great clumps of it burst from the undergrowth, beside prehistoric-looking ferns pressed against the damp earth.

To my right, Weobley Castle bathes itself in that apricot light, its bricks honeyed against the treetops. I'm not making a stop there today but I've hopped off my bike on the way past to explore it. It's worth a little visit.

The castle still looks almost exactly as it would have done 700 years ago, when the wealthy de la Bere family used this spot to build a fortified manor, intended for entertainment rather than war.

Inside, you'd have found the comforts of fourteenth-century privilege: a grand hall designed for spectacle, guest rooms with indoor latrines and a lord's solar,[26] which was a private retreat with thick walls and thin light, perfect for brooding in fancy velvet robes (i.e. a poet's ultimate dream). The military-style crenellations, watchtower, and imposing south-west turret hint however that if things went sideways, you could pour boiling oil on someone without leaving the comfort of your home.

Today, the castle peers down at the sheep, the saltmarsh, and the pheasants zipping between hedgerows. I wonder if it's noticed the lone runner pausing below the next ascent, a packet of Jelly Babies flattened to rainbow-coloured goo in her sports bra, feeling more than a little bit fed up.

★

I emerge, eventually, into Oldwalls. This is the location of another fancy wedding venue and not a part of Gower I frequent often. I'm not on the road long before I'm back into the woodland and can feel the unmistakable burning of my calves as I make a final climb, back up the scorched face of Cefn Bryn.

I glance at my live Strava map, which is still clinging to life at a risky 18% battery. Both of us are just trying to make it through by this point. Getting lost adds far more distance than planned, it turns out, and I'm fearful the sun will dissolve below the hill before I reach the top.

This is enough to force me to pick up the pace. I lurch forward until I'm out into bracken. My feet get soaked. I splash through the muddy water anyway. I don't even care anymore.

There's a moment – crouched awkwardly in the undergrowth, hands clawing at mud, hair full of twigs – where I actually consider staying there. Just stopping and letting the wilderness have me. I could become one of those tragic local myths: the ghost runner of Gower, last seen face-down in the bracken, trying to pause her Garmin.

By the halfway point, I am physically unravelled and emotionally fragile. My chest is heaving, my hands are filthy, and my thighs feel like they've been tenderised with a rolling pin. I honestly want to cry.

I've done longer, harder runs than this. It's just that emotions can be so tiring when you just want to stop and pour icy water into your mouth, then sleep. I think about hot showers. I think about soft pyjamas and thick, pliable pillows. I think about all the videos I could watch, rolled on my side in bed, of tiny piglets in amusing hats.

My blood sugars are still low. By now, my tongue feels fat and numb. It's like my legs aren't even there and I have no choice but to walk. I haven't got the energy to jump between boggy patches of mud and try to work out how to move forward without falling.

Another Jelly Baby meets its sorry fate in my mouth.

Cefn Bryn

★

At King Arthur's Stone, the light is a pure, brilliant orange. I point my phone towards it. I'm prepared to waste the last of my battery for this; I can see my car gleaming in the distance and I don't need the map anymore. I look down at the screen, scrutinising my efforts.

It's probably one of the better ones I've taken, but with only 5% battery left and the sun rapidly disappearing, I realise I should probably get a move on before I'm stranded on a Neolithic ridge with nothing but a dead GPS and four sweaty Jelly Babies for company.

Now at this point, I'd recommend jumping into the car or strolling down to the King Arthur pub for a very well-deserved pint and a pack of salty KP nuts.

However, when you're coated in sheep poo, have twigs in your bra and brambles in your hair, it's best not to scare the locals and just head on home.

Please enjoy your pint for me.

Llantwit Major

Location
Llantwit Major
SS 96741 68729

Distance
14K

Parking
Free parking at Llantwit Major Town Hall (blissfully quiet on a weekday morning).

Facilities
Grab an icy glass of water or a tall glass of lemonade at the Plough and Harrow, one of those delightfully olde-worlde pubs where you can easily get too comfortable before remembering you have to run back (to be honest, if it had been raining, I might have declared the run over right there, on a bar stool, penning a few lines).

Tips
Take road shoes for this one as it's all country lanes. For once, there is no peril of calf-deep mud or disgruntled livestock giving chase. It's all pretty civilised, actually.

Llantwit Major

Since taking up this curious habit of trail running and writing about it, I've found myself quietly stoking other creative fires. The writing has finally started flowing again and I've never been so delighted to be whipped up in its currents. As I drive into Llantwit Major, a gorgeous, sleepy little town that offers the same level of olde-worlde charm as Dinas Powys did, I'm plotting short stories in my head. It's been 10 years since I've written short stories seriously, but this process of long mornings out on the trails and making a commitment to writing has proved unexpectedly fruitful. Maybe it's just the sunshine, which puts me in a joyful mood, or it's the strange nostalgia of places like this, with its cobbled streets and Easter-egg-coloured buildings that remind me of childhood holidays.

Or maybe (and I'm starting to think this is it) there's actually something in letting yourself get a little bit lost and finding your way back again, whether that's to finally cross the finish line or to write your final paragraph.

Today I'm running with Bronwen, Seren's wonderful CEO. She's sharp, funny, and was the first person who gave me a platform to ramble on about writing and running, for which I'll always be grateful. Llantwit Major was her home and her place of healing for a while, so she knows these lanes and corners inside out, and I'm looking forward to seeing it through her eyes. I'm also very relieved to have a guide for once, which means no faffing about with maps or second-guessing turn-offs, then ending up in a hedge. I shove my phone into my bra, grateful to save the battery for the long, slow drive home.

We click the buttons on our watches and start running. It's

going to be a hot one today – only the faintest breeze scours the dry grass and herds move slowly, dozy in the warming air.

The first place of note we pass is St Illtud's Church (you'll remember this saint from the church at Oxwich, too), also known as the "Westminster Abbey of Wales" by the region's early rulers. These rulers (both secular and spiritual) left their mark in the form of inscribed stones; some etched with intricate Celtic patterns, others bearing Latin dedications. Some of these stones still survive today. It was founded by St Illtud in 500. This was once "one of the great international centres of Celtic Christianity, and one of the chief instruments by which Roman and European traditions were cherished in Welsh Wales".[27]

The western section of St Illtud's, built by the Normans, stands on the site of an earlier Celtic church, linking the medieval stone to the early Christian community that once flourished here. This part of the church served the spiritual needs of local residents for centuries, its current roof dating from the fifteenth century (in other words, I wouldn't recommend climbing on it). By contrast, the eastern section was constructed in the thirteenth century for the workers of the local monastic grange. This grange was land gifted by the powerful Norman lord, Robert Fitzhammon, and while this part of the church was more utilitarian, this didn't mean it was any less sacred in function. Together, these two halves formed a unique dual-purpose church. It's actually a pretty rare architectural arrangement that reflected the layered social and religious life of the time.[28]

Today, the church is still a hive of activity. Only yesterday, while scrolling Facebook to see what the local community were whingeing about this week ("What bins go out 2nite plz xx", "WHO HAS PARKED LIKE THIS, UTTERLY DISGUSTING"), I noticed an upcoming book launch happening at this very church. Scrolling farther back through its events calendar, I realised how central this place is to the community, particularly for artists of different mediums, with events for writers, musicians, and photographers, as well as the religious services.

After seeing the ruins of St Mary's Church back at Caerau Hill Fort, it's good to see places like this not only preserved but used to foster community spirit.

*

We're ascending the gently sloping Dimlands Road (which, while you're deep in conversation about local history, does leave you gasping just a little). Beside us, archways of trees open up as though slowly untwisting, giving way to rutted, gold fields and then snapping shut again, bathing us in shade. In the fields, cows lurch, their tiny bells coughing.

We talk about how we first got into running and why we decided to stick with it. One of the greatest joys I've gained so far from running these routes is the sheer variety of conversations I have along the way. Maybe it's even taught me that I'm not the antisocial lone runner I always thought I was, after all. It's not all about pace and performance metrics; sometimes, it's about why someone insists on pounding the same stretch of canal path every week, then finding out there's a deep nostalgia that keeps them returning. Everyone has different reasons that reveal a little more about who they are. Some are reconnecting with memories. Some are pulling themselves back together and finding the routes that heal them. Others are indeed competitive, and love the thrill of hammering up and down the most challenging terrains. There's never a running story that's entirely the same: everyone's running towards or away from something. And I absolutely get it.

But what links so many stories is how running makes us feel. We discuss running as a healer, a head-clearer, or the agitation when we haven't pulled on our running shoes in a few days. How it becomes not just positive, but necessary.

Both of us have felt healing through running, and for Bronwen, this is the route that brought her back to herself, in the same way mine is along Loughor Estuary (more on that one later in the book).

The road opens out on our left to a vast field and tangled hedges, in stark contrast to the ordered flowerbeds and meticulously-arranged hanging baskets on our right. In thick windows the sunlight takes hold, reflecting our shapes back at us in brief flashes of vibrantly-striped running tights.

'Does someone actually live there?' I ask, gesturing towards a miniature castle squatting alongside the road. It looked like a leftover prop from a particularly lavish children's birthday party, or perhaps the plastic fort my sister and I once forced our Barbies to repel invasions from.

'Yes, that's what's left of Dimlands House,' Bronwen informs me. 'Just the castellated lodge. Gorgeous, isn't it?' It is. It looks like somewhere Henry VIII would run a poetry retreat (if Henry VIII ran poetry retreats). Dimlands House was built in the late eighteenth century by the Rev Robert Nicholl Carne. Born nearby at Ham House, Robert inherited 99 acres upon his father's death and raised a "gentleman's" residence – i.e. spacious, dignified, with a Tudor staircase and two drawing rooms (sounds like a pretty nice house for a lady, too, I'd argue. I'd love waltzing through two drawing rooms in a silk dressing gown). Carne was an antiquarian at heart, penning early histories of Llantwit Major. In 1798, a hoard of Roman silver was unearthed in Eglyws-Brewis, which he kept in his possession. Robert died in 1849, and Dimlands passed to his son John, born in the house but living then at Tresilian. In the 1850s, John transformed the place, adding a porch, a library, Minton tiles, and a castellated lodge which is what remains today.

When John died, it was leased to a number of local worthies until it destroyed by a fire in 1948.[29] There's almost something a little Brontë-esque about it.

We continue up onwards, ribboning through the green-slung branches of Dimlands Road. Just past the gnarled wrists of bramble hedgerows and cow-parsley, there's a hint of coast glittering beyond the edge of the field like a strip of steel laid down at the sky's hem. The air is thick with the scent of farmland and damp stone, a reminder of how Llantwit's location near the coast and its fertile lands supported a thriving agricultural economy for years.

To our right, there are some gorgeous (and expensive) looking houses, closing in on an abandoned swimming pool. Bronwen informs me that this is Tresilian Bay House, named after the third- or fourth-century Celtic Prince Silian (possibly, but not confirmed). Once upon a time, it doubled as an inn, complete with a bathing lodge. This is the slightly eerie-looking pool in front of us today. Later, in the mid-nineteenth century, it became a private residence for the Stradling-Carne family and was later let to tenants: the Morells (Cardiff shipowners), a farmer named David Williams, then Owen and Barbara Crawshay (née Carne), and their daughter Sylvia who were buried just down the lane in the churchyard at St Donat's, marked in weathered stone and, more recently, in the village postmaster's history book.

There's a rumour that in around 1940, in the midst of World War Two, Haile Selassie, the exiled Emperor of Ethiopia, was given house protection here. Later, the house was lived in by the Shaw family, then Barbara Woodhouse, the dog trainer of BBC fame. In 1953, Eric and Pamela Jones (Popular Plastics, Bridgend) bought the house and grounds and the family have occupied it ever since.

But the most enduring story clinging to the place belongs to Sir Henry Stradling of St Donat's Castle. According to local legend, Sir Henry was kidnapped by pirates and held hostage until his father paid a king's ransom.

The boy came home, but he didn't forget.

The rest of his life became a kind of reckoning as he pursued the men who'd taken him to get his revenge. One of them, a man known only as Pete, was found years later, hiding in the dark slit of a cave at Tresilian Bay. Stradling's men dragged him to a rock pool and drowned him there. The tide didn't even have to help.

They say his ghost lingers still, in the silence of Reynard's Cave. Sometimes, they say, you can hear him, deep in the yawning dark.

I shiver and move on.

*

The road turns slightly and we see a sign for Atlantic College, set in St Donat's Castle. Now, this one has a background that really surprised me. Before it was founded as an educational institution by Dr Kurt Hahn in 1962, it was the seaside playground of the American newspaper magnate William Randolph Hearst (yes, Citizen Kane, which he hated by the way). He spotted the place in *Country Life* (as one does) and promptly bought it in 1925 (as you do). His lavish parties at the 60-hectare estate were legendary with guests such as Charlie Chaplin, Sir Douglas Fairbanks, future president John F Kennedy and his family, and playwright George Bernard Shaw.[30]

I'm beyond impressed; I can barely drag more than two mates over for a barbecue.

It's weird to stand there, sweating slightly under the dappled shade, knowing who was here before you. Like you've walked into a paused film and everyone left the room. To an outsider, the Welsh coast has always played the part of a moody seductress in a windswept gothic novel: jagged cliffs, flotsam-streaked steps, and ruined chapels gazing out to sea. I suppose it's where poets go to think too much and filmmakers go to brood in slow motion. Dylan Thomas described the "sloeblack, slow, black, crowblack, fishingboatbobbing sea" in his famous *Under Milk Wood*, while BBC period dramas have turned every bay into a plausible setting for a slow-burning love affair or a deeply significant death by drowning. Perhaps Hearst didn't just buy a house. He bought the narrative.

*

Llantwit Major

At one point, I'm slightly startled by Easter Island-type faces and huge fibreglass cows beside the water at a place called Gribbles Covert, believing them to be real. I make a mental note to stop ignoring my Specsavers letters. This stretch of water, once popular with anglers, is remarkably peaceful. I imagine a silvery carp moving beneath the water's surface, turning its sleek body toward us. If a few lines of poetry were going to pop into my head, it's during this brief lull:

> *Everywhere, the air is thick with the hush:*
> *sap-fug, fern-sweat, the occasional laugh*
> *of a distant bird losing its mind on the water.*

It's uphill from here, gently, a mist of nettles bordering thick hedgerows and fields of churned earth. We pass several disused agricultural buildings, remnants of Llantwit Major's important status as a farming community (in fact, the 1851 and 1861 censuses show that the main occupation was that of agricultural labourer). Though there are working farms here still, it is not at the sheer scale it used to be.

When we reach Marcross, there's a turning for Nash Point Lighthouse. If you've got time and want a longer run, do go and have a look (and get some stunning photos, too). Beneath the Bristol Channel's choppy waves lies a graveyard of wrecks, none more infamous than *The Frolic*, a doomed steam vessel swallowed by Nash Sands in 1831, taking 78 lives with it. You'll remember the smuggler tales from Oxwich I mentioned earlier in the book. Well, they were up to their usual tricks here, too: tying lanterns to sheep (I told you not to trust sheep) to mimic ships in safe waters, luring unsuspecting vessels to their doom. Nash Point Lighthouse was one of two lighthouses built by Trinity House in 1832 to successfully assist mariners clear of the Nash Sands. [31] The tragedy of *The Frolic* was the last of its kind to happen here before these lighthouses were built.

Bronwen is keen to show me one of her old favourite pubs, The Horseshoe Inn, but once we get there, there's nothing to see except boarded-up windows and paint flaking like fish-scales, curled from the lintel. The benches sprout nettles, rusted brackets still clenched in the wall, knuckle-tight. The hanging baskets swing, with nothing inside them but the wind. It all looks quite sad. You can tell this would have once been a pleasant spot for an afternoon drink, tucked in the countryside and in the perfect spot for the best of the sunshine.

We still get our drink, but farther along the road. Once we reach Monknash, The Plough and Harrow is there to welcome us in, utterly deserted apart from a cheerful man who greets us as he readies the pub for the day. We sit outside for a while, basking in the sun's warmth, sipping chilled lemonade and iced water. The Plough and Harrow is one of those stone-walled, oak-doored establishments that seems trapped in a time far older than this, with its original stone walls, thick wooden doors, and a deep fireplace.

Turns out, that's because it *is* old. Far older than I even imagined, in fact; it dates back to 1383. You know those rogues I mentioned earlier who would trick ships into steering towards the deadly Nash sandbank? There was once a partitioned chamber in this pub that was used to store the shipwrecked bodies washed up on the beach.[32] The pub and its surroundings are said to be crawling with ghosts. And apparently, these ones get pretty hands-on: tugging at the staff, rearranging the furniture, and holding full-blown conversations in an otherwise empty bar (no word on whether they buy a round).

Fortunately, my drink doesn't start shifting down the table on its own, so maybe the ghosts are busy with pot wash duties today.

Originally, we were going to turn around and head back from this point, but it's such a stunning spring morning it's not hard to convince ourselves to keep going a little farther. Suitably refreshed after a cold drink and a toilet break, we continue onwards. Now, if you want to add a bit of sea air to your route, you can turn off through Blaen y Cwm Nature Reserve and down to the coast. We decide to continue up the hill instead, to take in the old monastic grange that I'm quite curious about.

It's hot now. Any remaining clouds have peeled away to reveal the dazzlingly sharp sunlight. A pearl of sweat runs from my temple to my chin and I can taste the salt along my lips. Thank God we stopped for water because without it, I'd be cramping up like a damp dishrag left out to dry. There's no shade along this stretch; it's all open road, wide fields, and barely a shudder of breeze to take the edge off.

Bronwen stops and points out the remains of the grange. I imagine this would have once been a grand, sprawling scene, busy with activity. This was once the domain of Tewkesbury Abbey in Neath, and was the richest farm they owned. The grange grew to become like a small town with a church, living quarters, college, forge, carpenter's workshop, tithe barn, trout pools, dove cotes and animal buildings (it was practically Centre Parcs for monks). Now, it's a shadow of its former self: uneven hollows and toppled walls that hint at a previous life that quietly slipped beneath the moss long ago.

It's time to turn back the way we came. And honestly, I'm fine to take it all in again in reverse. After a week of work conferences, deadlines, and feeling more than a little frazzled, Llantwit Major is the remedy I needed.

Need to clear your head and shake off the stress? Want a route that has so much more to it than it ever gives away? Put this route in your running plan. 14 kilometres later, I *completely* understand how this place can be so healing.

Pen Pych

Location
Pen Pych, near Treorchy
SS 92440 99119

Distance
7K

Parking
Plenty of parking at Pen Pych Forest car park. And even better, it's free.

Facilities
Lots of little cafes on the nearby High Street for post-run refreshments (and, if you're anything like me, people-watching over an espresso).

Tips
Despite the last kilometre being on-road, I still recommend you bring trail shoes. The downwards stretch requires a bit of footwork if you're going at speed. Also, if you can, clamber over the rocks towards the waterfall and enjoy the view. It's absolutely worth it.

Pen Pych

If you've ever driven to the Brecon Beacons via Rhondda, you've probably swept past this place without a second glance. Which is fine really, because the more people do this, the more peaceful it is when you finally discover it. I only know about this one because I was dragged up here once on a hike and was quite enchanted by it, so I feel excited to return and share this one with you now. There's absolutely no doubt that the climb to the top is going to feel a lot more intense at running pace, but mentally, I'm feeling prepared. After all, many hills have been overcome prior to this one (Pen y Fan, I'm looking at you).

The drive up is, mercifully, almost pleasurable, which is a rare luxury after countless M4 treks where the scenery so often blurs into motorway signage and the flash of impatient overtakers. The road up through Rhigos Mountain offers a visual feast of hulking pines, rugged hillsides, and deep valleys. Ted is with me today and it's on this mountain road that he strains towards the window, mesmerised, at the wind turbines plonked on the top of the hills like vast skeletal pinwheels scything through the skyline. I stare, equally mesmerised, at the procession of cyclists grinding up the incline ahead of me.

While I might have tackled some difficult turbo trainer challenges this week, it doesn't compare to the monumental effort of these cyclists. After all, Zwift doesn't throw crosswinds at you or present you with a Ford Fiesta doing 60 in the wrong lane. Having to navigate traffic and battle against the wind direction is a very different ball game and I have nothing but respect for these Saturday morning thrill-seekers.

I shift my car into a lower gear and let it carry us, shuddering, onwards.

Wild Running

It's already warm this morning as I pull into Pen Pych Forest car park. It's early enough that the only sounds are a wren heckling from the brambles, its voice huge in its soft chest, and the gentle shiver of breeze through pine. The air is damp, but feels clean, as though it's been rinsed by rainfall overnight.

I jump out of the car, eager to find inspiration. Ted strains at his leash, eager to find things to pee on.

★

The route begins through the forest, climbing gently through a well-maintained trail lined with pine and larch. The scent is sharp and resinous. I let it distract me, momentarily, from the sharp pain that jolts through my tibia with every smack of my right heel against the earth. My shin splints, much to my irritation, have been getting steadily worse.

This is going to be more of a limp than a run, which is unfortunate, because Ted is ready to set a world sprinting record.

The gravel path zig zags through the trees and I can't help but notice how many new paths have been formed by people taking shortcuts. I learned a few years ago that these are called 'desire lines', which poets obviously love (I mean, it's a title and a poem right there in front of you). I'm determined to not get lost today, so I stick to the original path even though I can see where the desire lines emerge. I'm simply not taking any risks because I've got a route and I intend to follow it. I don't do shortcuts.

I am, let me be clear, a very serious runner.

I feel closed in, hidden almost, by the mountains rising around me. It's not suffocating; it's actually weirdly comforting. There's no one else here apart from me and my tiny Jack Russell, and I feel both completely alone and intensely observed, if that makes sense. Had this been one of the popular waterfall routes in Brecon, the car parks would already be full and the paths jammed with hikers. For today, I'm happy with this level of quietness. The last few weeks have been a blur of deadlines, work trips, and submissions, along with some just-about-squeezed-in social events. If it's not been too many screens, it's been too much talking, so the silence, for today, is just what I needed to soothe my chattering brain. My skin feels like there are spiders running in quick little circles everywhere.

It happens a lot when my calendar gets a little too busy. The funny thing is, people assume that if you read your work in public, you must be a natural extrovert, constantly fizzing with ideas and your confidence pouring out like the cheap prosecco at your latest book launch.

Yet I'm the opposite.

I am, at heart, a pretty textbook introvert. My idea of a good time is putting on fresh pyjamas and opening a new book, borderline suffocating with the aroma of the moderately-priced sandalwood candle sputtering on the mantelpiece. I'd rather read poetry alone in the bath than read it publicly to a crowd while wearing an uncomfortable yet fashionable dress.

But what I never knew before I became a writer is that it requires performance; whether that's at panels, on air, at launches, in rooms where you're expected to sparkle and live up to a persona you've constructed for yourself. This persona is often necessary. It becomes a second skin, one that fits better on some days than others. It's not fake, but it's still a costume. And like any costume, it gets uncomfortable if you keep it on for too long.

Whether you're a teacher, a nurse, a barista, an artist, a manager, or someone just trying to make it through another social gathering without imploding, it's likely you have your own costume too. You might wear it to sound more confident than you feel, more agreeable, more upbeat, or more capable. Sometimes this is good (fake it till you make it, right?). And often, it's not. Running takes me out of this persona and back to myself. When I run, I don't need to explain myself. I'm not performing. I'm not marketing the next book or event. I'm not "on". My body leads and my brain is allowed to simply follow, or drift, or unravel, however it likes.

So many of us are carrying versions of ourselves we built to survive, whether that's at work, in friendships, or in rooms that don't make space for our quiet parts. It's okay to step out of that skin sometimes. Not everything has to be a performance, and you're allowed to be a little undone and a little off-stage.

I slip over a rock and come back to myself, hands covered in tiny stones.

I can swear as loudly as I want; there's no one around to hear it.

★

As we climb upwards, I can see the village of Blaencwm, a scatter of tiny buildings in the scoop of the valley, tucked tight against the hip of Pen Pych Mountain.

What's easy to miss is that this modest village once stood at the mouth of industry. Blaencwm was the northern entrance to the Taff Vale Railway tunnel, built in 1890, an important railway line that connected the coal-rich Rhondda with the ports of Swansea Bay. The tons of coal that were shifted every week powered factories, cities, and lives far beyond the valleys. Then, in the 1960s – like so many of the old lines and stations – it was closed and left to the dark. Today, there are campaigns to try and bring it back, not for trains this time, but for people. Campaigners hope to reopen it as the longest underground cycle lane in Europe and it's even got the support of the brilliant Michael Sheen.

There's something oddly moving about knowing what once thundered beneath your feet. I mean, it could also just be that I'm very hormonal this week, but so often on these runs it's the history and the stories of these places that have really helped me to connect with the landscapes that have held me within them. Coal, sweat, and real, working people once funnelled through that tunnel to power a world beyond this valley. And now, decades later, people want to cycle through it in Lycra. It feels both beautiful and slightly surreal.

Pen Pych

I think about how my old physics teacher once told me that energy never really disappears, it just changes form. Maybe that's what this place is doing too: transforming.

*

It doesn't take long to reach the first waterfall, but if the climb had me out of breath when walking it before then it has me wheezing when running. On some parts, I do have to slow to a walk. My ankles twist into bizarre angles. My hands, more than once, hit the floor to steady myself.

Ted sees it before I do. To be honest, I should really have relieved myself before the start of this run because the sound of rushing water, meditative though it is, is not helping my bladder situation. He's already wriggling down through branches and onto a narrow path just to the left of us, heading towards the sound.

Being just as curious, I follow.

We don't quite make it to the waterfall itself, but we get close. I find two flat-ish stones, wedge a foot on each, and crouch to watch the water foaming down the rockface and into the refreshingly clear pool beneath us. Ted, meanwhile, dabbles his paws delicately at the edge, stares at me with solemn intent, then promptly lifts his leg and pees on a nearby fallen tree.

I swear he's trying to make me jealous.

We re-emerge onto the path and find ourselves facing some steep-looking steps. I slow to a light jog; the morning air is thickening with heat. Ted sprints up and down impatiently, pausing only to check whether I'm following or dead.

For the first time on this walk, we aren't alone. A woman reclines on one of the flat, silvery rocks beside Berw Wion waterfall, looking out over the horizon and breathing deeply. Being courteous, she moves when she sees me and tells me to enjoy the sunshine. I tell her she doesn't need to go, but I have a feeling Ted would have put an end to her moment of tranquillity.

He is flinging himself over the large slabs of rock in excited circles, tongue flapping from his jaw.

I'm being treated today. When I saw this waterfall before, it was a little overcast, though still scenic. Today, with the cloudless sky, the sun pours through the glassy water to create a miniature rainbow, suspended between rock and pool. I sit and watch it for a while, mesmerised by this perfect angle of sunlight and water. Of course I take a photo. Of course I scribble a few lines of poetry into my phone:

> *A thin, impossible loop*
> *burned into spray:*
> *the rainbow flaring briefly,*
> *optical trickster,*
> *a mirage you could kneel to.*

I'm kneeling now, not to worship, but to get a decent photo of Ted looking cute watching the water twisting itself like a white strand from the mountain's scalp. He looks vaguely philosophical against the backdrop of the tumbling water, his head slightly tilted as if pondering the impermanence of nature. It's more likely that he's wondering whether he can eat a rock.

I offer him a drink from his collapsible bowl and take a long swig from my own bottle. It's barely 9am and the heat is plastering my pink running top to my back like clingfilm. Ted begins to pant. The adrenaline of the scent trail has worn off and we're both ready for some shade.

We head back towards the path, letting the branches close over us, then push onwards.

★

The climb isn't as difficult as I remember it, which I'm very pleased about; all this recent business of hauling myself up hills in the name of fitness, mindfulness, or whatever else I told myself at the time, is beginning to pay off. We're almost at the summit of Pen Pych Mountain, which sounds like a really impressive thing to tell people you've done before breakfast. Now, what makes this place truly special is that Pen Pych is one of only two tabletop spur mountains in the whole of Europe, making it pretty geologically unique. It doesn't rise as high as Wales's headliners, but standing at 442m it still offers spectacular views over Blaencwm and Blaenrhondda. I pause a while at the top, looking down over the valleys. Ted is still more mesmerised by the wind turbines on the hills. He stands beside me, ears pricked, watching them slice the air.

Stillness, for me, has always felt suspicious. But actually, now that I've run so many of these beautiful trails, I realise that maybe I've just found the closest thing to meditation I can do. It's started to show positive effects in other areas of my life. Yes, I'm slightly frazzled and dashing between events, sending out submissions, and trying to write things people will want to read without hating every word on the page. These trails – and it's so obvious now when I think back over the last few months – have really rewired something. I can say that with certainty.

I've convinced myself I'm going to lose my job for no reason whatsoever other than overthinking and misinterpreting Slack messages that don't contain enough smiley face emojis. I've cried over a rejection or two, despite myself. I've celebrated shortlistings for literary competitions, then days later, found myself in an absolute panic waiting for an email to tell me that it was a mistake. Either that, or I've been consumed by guilt that I simply don't deserve it.

But since doing all this, it's been easier to observe those thoughts and not react immediately. And isn't that what they always tell you to do when you're meditating? I often find that if I sit still (upright, comfy pillow, trying to ignore a random itch in my arse cheek), my mind throws thoughts at me to ruin it. I can't observe those thoughts. There are just too many of them.

When I'm running, I feel what I need to feel. I acknowledge it. I keep going. The thought stays for a while, then disappears, like it got bored waiting for me to react.

I've since learned that when you're deeply involved in any activity, you're meditative. A 2016 study published in *Translational Psychiatry* found that combining directed meditation with running or walking reduced symptoms of depression by 40% for depressed participants, and more research is ongoing.[33] That steady rhythm – footfall after footfall – creates a kind of mental entrainment, giving the mind something consistent to focus on, like breath in yoga or a mantra in meditation.

I'm certainly not saying it's a miracle cure. Running doesn't simply "fix" depression. That kind of thinking is dangerous, and to be honest, insulting to anyone who's experienced the painful, unrelenting nature of it. But it can be a part of your mental health toolkit. It can sit alongside other tools like medication, therapy, and support systems as part of the bigger picture of managing your mental health. Running, for me, sits in my toolkit as part of it, and not as the whole solution. If I didn't take medication, I probably wouldn't be able to get out of bed to run at all.

Even elite runners talk about this. In *Running with the Mind of Meditation,* Sakyong Mipham,[34] a Tibetan lama and marathoner, explores how mindful running can become a spiritual practice; not by disconnecting from the body, but by anchoring into it fully. The point is, you don't transcend during a run.

You come back to yourself.

*

Good news: there's no more climbing from here onwards. It's wonderfully flat then tips even more wonderfully downhill. Now, I recommend trail shoes for this next bit. Shin splints and a sore knee are bad enough, but it's the loose, uneven rocks waiting to dislocate your ankle that are the real menace here.

I'd also like to add, proudly, that I've not got lost yet. I haven't even got a live map going. I just have a screenshot of a map I glance at every now and then, and – get this – *I can read it.* I actually *know* which way the paths are going and which way I'm facing. In fact, I spend the next ten minutes constructing a whole fantasy life in which I lead a dramatic Arctic expedition with nothing but a compass, a sensible fleece, and the ability to remain calm while others panic. I rescue fellow adventurers with a single glance at topography. I say things like, "The ridge curves northeast; we'll drop into the valley at first light," while sipping strong coffee I've skilfully brewed over a tiny stove.

The air cools slightly, pine-scented and shaded, and I start to think about breakfast. All I've brought with me is a slightly squashed cereal bar made of peanuts and dates. I start to feel unreasonably sad about it.

Eventually, we hear water again. It's the final straw for my bladder. I glance behind me, check for witnesses, and then creep off the path and into the trees with all the stealth and shame of someone committing a countryside offence. At last, sighing deeply, I relieve my bladder behind a reassuringly thick tree trunk.

Ted does the same for the 453rd time on this walk. We share the relief, admiring the stream beside us as it twists through the dappled shade.

We carry on, down through the trees. The forest paths keep tempting us off-course but we stick to the plan. I've made it this far without getting lost, and I'm not about to ruin my flawless record now. For the first time, my Strava route is going to be marvellously, perfectly circular with no detours.

We eventually reach a quiet road and I put Ted back on his lead. He's panting again now, so maybe it's time for us both to walk for the last kilometre. He's tired and my shins feel like they're going to explode. We continue on, slowly under the glare of the sun and catch sight of a strange little arrangement of stone structures.

This is Fernhill Colliery, which was sunk by Ebenezer Lewis around 1870 at the head of the Rhondda Fawr valley. Men walked into it every day with sandwiches wrapped in newspaper and walked out again sore, stained, but still joking. An information sign reveals that at its peak, the colliery had five shafts and employed nearly 2,000 men. It was a hive of industrial activity for over 100 years.

Caroline Street was also here, which housed the workers and their families. The street was named after Caroline, Countess of Dunraven, whose family land the colliery was built on. The families who lived here formed a tight-knit community until the houses were demolished in 1973 and the people moved to new houses further down the valley.

Without reading this sign, I never would have guessed that this is a place where people would have pulled each other through hardships and celebrated the good times. There's little left but rock, grass and the brief streak of a crow lifting into the air.

*

We're into the little village of Blaenrhondda now, which is starting to wake up with dog walkers and squealing children bouncing footballs over the tarmac. The odd radio blares a breakfast show through a cracked kitchen window and someone is frying bacon. I think sadly, again, about my cereal bar.

We're not far from where we started, and the mountain already feels distant, as if it were a different version of the day. One minute you're halfway up a mountain, your quads clenching and the sky opening up around you, and the next you're stepping over a drain cover, watching a child drop a Fruit Shoot on the pavement. Both of these things are real. Both of these things can inspire writing.

> *I am not who I was at the summit,*
> *legs heavy, pockets*
> *crammed with pine needles.*
> *There's a woman in a dressing gown*
> *watering her concrete,*
> *still holding the shape of the night.*

I tell Ted we're nearly at the car. I promise him a treat: a twisted, bacon-scented thing that's probably got all greasy in my car by now. Ted doesn't understand a word I'm saying, but he looks up at me as though he does. My legs have taken on the texture of overcooked linguine, and my water bottle, now warm, gives one final glug. Ted and I have gone through two bottles between us.

We're both thinking about the nap we'll have when we get home. We're warm, we're tired, but we're pretty bloody happy.

We share a squashed cereal bar in the car park while I look at photos of rainbows.

Tintern Abbey

Location
Tintern Abbey, Wye Valley
SO 53282 00131

Distance
8K

Parking
Parking available outside Tintern Abbey. Get there early though if going on a warm day – it's a popular spot for a weekend walk.

Facilities
You're spoilt for choice near at the start and end of the run, with The Anchor Inn, White Monk Tea Rooms, and Filling Station Cafe all near the car park. There are toilets too, which, I've learned, is something of a luxury on a trail route.

Tips
Hot day? Try the raspberry ripple ice cream from White Monk Tea Rooms then sit outside to people-watch with the Abbey looming dramatically in the background.

Tintern Abbey

I've been arguing with myself since 9am, not wanting to run, but still perched on the edge of the bed debating it in my head while clutching a coffee and staring emptily at the window. It takes until 11am to finally drag myself out of my pyjamas, into my running gear, and into the car for one hour and forty minutes of soul-crushing motorway driving.

(If, by the time you are holding this book in your hand, you are somehow aware that I've not fixed the air conditioning in my car yet, you are absolutely allowed to scream at me.)

It's a long, sweaty drive along the M4, but I remind myself that I'm nearly done with the runs for this book. I sweat through Bridgend. I stew through Cardiff. By Newport I'm convinced I am actual soup. There's a small satisfaction in passing the signs for Caerphilly and Cardiff and Margam, and I think about the routes I've done so far. All wildly different, but all an incredible way to uncover the gems we have in South Wales and remind me of how much I love living here and how much I love running.

I find myself wishing I had company. It's too hot and too far today for Ted. Ian, when I asked him to join me, just laughed, which meant, "I'd rather saw my own legs off, thanks." My music washes over my head, barely registered as I mentally put my deadlines in order and try not to piss anyone off when changing lanes. It was too last-minute to rope anyone else in, so I sigh and stare out and count down the junctions. I'm driving so far east that I begin to worry I'll somehow overshoot Wales entirely and end up in Gloucestershire by accident, so it reassures me to see Welsh words on the road signs as I near Tintern.

It is, as I expected, hectic today. The car park grumbles with engines as people prowl slowly in their vehicles, hoping to dive into a space at the right moment. I'm lucky. Just as I'm turning in, someone pulls out of a space directly in front of me and I almost remove my hands from the steering wheel to punch the air in victory.

A man glares at me and revs angrily past. 'You snooze, you lose,' I whisper to myself, killing the engine and placing my headphones over my ears like a ceremonial crown.

*

The photo opportunities on this route start pretty much instantly. I've barely got both legs out of the car before I'm snapping pictures of the Abbey towering over the car park, gazing up with the rest of the crowd. A man wearing socks and flip-flops reads the information sign loudly to his wife, who looks as though she is only half-listening. A shih tzu pees against a wall that was once holy. Somewhere behind me, someone small drops an ice cream and screams.

I'm here far too late in the day to enjoy a peaceful run, so I brace myself for tripping over dogs and dodging swinging picnic baskets.

Tintern Abbey has long been abandoned by all things holy, but it's still a national icon; hollowed out and missing its roof, but it's still a place of ethereal beauty and photogenic melancholy. It was founded in 1131 by Cistercian monks who, like many of the holy men we've encountered so far, started small. They were more than happy with their mere timber buildings at first. Abbot Henry, a reformed robber, was better known for his habit of crying at the altar than for his architectural ambitions.[35] Eventually, money arrived thanks to the generous backing of the wealthy Marcher Lords. With patronage came progress, and in 1269 the monks set about building a proper abbey church. They didn't stop until they'd produced one of the great Gothic showpieces of British monastic architecture.

Tintern Abbey

The west front, with its soaring seven-lancet window, still draws gasps from day-trippers, even if, like me, they have no idea what a lancet window is.

Gratitude in the medieval period took the form of prayers, alms, and naming rights. The monks remained loyally grateful to their benefactor, Roger Bigod, well into the sixteenth century and were still handing out alms on his behalf in 1535, long after he'd departed the scene. Sadly, it didn't save them. By 1536, Henry VIII's English Reformation was in full swing, and Tintern was one of the first abbeys to fall in the dissolution of the monasteries. The monks left. The roof collapsed. Wind whistled through the abbey's wasted bones.

Today, it's both a day trip destination and an aesthetic backdrop for moody social media posts with quotes from Rilke or Taylor Swift. It may no longer be sacred in the technical sense, but it's still silently admired by visitors like me, crouching behind the protective fence to get the most dramatic angle for their Instagram stories.

★

There's a bit of weaving between people in sun hats and swinging tote bags before I reach the bridge into the woods, giving spectacular views over the River Wye. This is the Wireworks Bridge, built in 1876 to link the railway with the Lower Wireworks site in Tintern. However, I later learn that the construction of this bridge turned out to be bad timing, arriving just in time for the tail end of the industrial boom, when enthusiasm for heavy metalwork was beginning to wane and nobody particularly needed it anymore. So, during that time, it was barely used.

Fast forward a century and a half, and suddenly this bridge has found its second act. Now, hundreds of people cross it daily to get back to the gift shop or start their walk through the Wye Valley woodlands towards Devil's Pulpit or the Offa's Dyke path. If this bridge feels oddly familiar, by the way, that's because the Wireworks Bridge had its big break in Netflix's *Sex Education* (yes, even cooler than *Countryfile*).

The sun is fiercely hot during this lunchtime run, so I'm grateful to be swallowed in the cover of woodland on the other side of the bridge. It's busy. There's a woman behind me who coughs often, so I time my steps to her until we're a weird little duet. A boy drops an apple and his family, scattered on a picnic blanket, watch as it rolls perfectly into the shadow of a log.

My heart rate, I notice, is far higher than it usually is for such a relaxed pace. The stress has been mounting, so as I bounce along the dry earth, I thank my stubborn self this morning for dragging myself out on this run. My overwhelming desire over the past couple of weeks has been to ignore everything and pull the duvet over myself like an enormous, wriggling, human larva. I can feel the warning signs and know it's time to get a handle on the stress. Staying in 'creator' mode all the time is difficult and I've learned that it's simply not how the cycle of creative seasons work.

However, sitting and watching my content briefs and writing deadlines as they build up isn't going to get any bills paid.

Stress is a message. And if you can bear to sit with it (or run with it), it will tell you exactly what you need to know. So for now, I will simply run, and let it peel back, layer by layer, until I find the source and what needs to change.

I hope that when you need it, running will give you the respite you're looking for, too.

★

Above me, the trees ruffle with crows. The light shifts in long, bruised slants, striping my arms to reveal the terrible job I've done of trying to blend my sun cream. I look like a badly-iced cake.

The breathtaking natural scenery here has enthralled visitors for centuries, including painters and poets from Turner to Wordsworth[36], and I can see why. Wyndcliff Wood makes

Tintern Abbey

me feel like I'm running through the set of *Robin Hood*, and I probably wouldn't bat an eyelid if the Merry Men strolled past me, singing. According to Joseph Bradney, this woodland gets its name from the Welsh words *Chwyth gwynt*, meaning "the blowing of the wind", which was recorded by Nennius (a Welsh monk of the ninth century) as *Huit gwynt*. This, he suggests, is the true origin of the modern name, rather than it being a combination of the words "Wye" and "cliff".

Soon, I'm greeted with the sight of a precarious-looking climb over some rocks, which takes a bit of careful footwork. My advice here is to stick to the right at the start of the climb rather than on the smoother section of the rock if you don't want to end up sprawled in the dirt, trying to remember the phone number of your most trusted emergency contact. Something about this steep woodland climb reminds me of the steps in Oxwich, that other sadistic staircase of a trail that masqueraded as a nice jog through the woods. As my calves and glutes begin to squeeze and burn, I slow down to a light jog and then a walk, puffing as my heart rate hovers in the 160s. I'm struggling today. I have an overwhelming desire to curl up in the shade and nap.

Ahead of me, three small boys leap over the steps, making easy work of it even with their little legs. Their parents push on, slightly breathless, taking measured strides. I decide I need to save face as someone who's come here to run; in other words, I cannot possibly allow myself to fall behind a toddler in Crocs. I smile at the parents as I pass them, attempting to look casual, like I do this sort of thing all the time and I'm not in the slightest bit out of breath. As soon as they've dropped out of sight, I find a steady tree trunk, lean against it and pant furiously. Why do I do this to myself? I massage my calves to try and get the muscles to unclench.

Frilling the edge of the pathway, garlic flowers pepper the earth like stray confetti. I breathe among them deeply as I pause, inhaling the earthy sweetness. I've grown to love this scent.

The incline becomes less steep, but it's still a climb, though perhaps a little more forgivably undulating in parts. The woodland is dense and dark, revealing nothing so far of what I know will be a spectacular view across the Wye Valley. But the views *are* coming, I promise.

In the meantime, I'm pausing more frequently. This route is far hillier than I expected. Hills are often the part of trail running we most love to hate, until of course, we learn about how effective and beneficial they are. They might feel like punishment in the moment, but persevere and hill training will become one of your biggest allies in building speed, strength, and resilience. From a physiological standpoint, running uphill demands greater muscle activation than running on flat terrain, particularly in the glutes, hamstrings, calves, and quadriceps. And then there's the cardiovascular benefit. Hills naturally push your heart rate higher in short bursts, mimicking interval training and stimulating aerobic capacity without needing to do speed drills on a track (good news if you find running in circles mind-numbing). A 2013 study published in the *International Journal of Sports Physiology and Performance* looked at runners who completed six weeks of high-intensity uphill intervals. The results showed improvements not only in running economy (meaning they used less energy to maintain pace) but also in performance, with participants averaging 2% faster times in 5K trials. The researchers concluded that incorporating high-intensity uphill intervals is a reliable way for runners to enhance their 5K race performance.[37]

So, there you have it. The pain of a brutal hill is actually a good thing if you want to be a better runner.

★

Eventually, I reach the summit and see a small sign engraved upon a stone in the ground: *Devil's Pulpit*. Which, to be honest, sounds like the name of a band I'd probably go and see.

When I look up, the view through the trees is something special. Framed by dark branches, the abbey sprawls below me, its bones exposed: vaulted ribs, high arches, a spine of rustling grass. Cars swing up the road like shimmering beetles. And beside it all, the River Wye, slow-ribboned and pewter, winds its way through the knees of the hills.

> *It lounges across the valley,*
> *one hip pressed to the bank,*
> *water dark with old holiness*
> *and last night's rain.*

It felt like the right time for a quick poetic scribble. I have a power bank attached to my phone now, so I'm less jumpy about the battery situation. If I want to write poetry, check my blood sugars in my app, and take a picture, I can do all of these things in the knowledge that my phone won't die and leave me stranded on a hillside, weeping.

So, where does the 'Devil's Pulpit' name come from?

According to local legend, the Devil himself picked this rocky stage to deliver sermons of his own, hoping to lure the monks of Tintern away from God and into whatever chaos he had in mind. One version even has him proposing to preach a lewd and blasphemous sermon from the Abbey roof (the little scamp). The monks, however, were apparently wise to his antics so they simply played along. They let him scramble up and then, at the perfect moment, they doused him with holy water and sent him packing.

While the view is stunning and the limestone geology is impressive, it's the image of a slightly soggy Devil slipping off medieval stonework in a fit of utter embarrassment that really makes the climb worth it.

Once I've had my fill of gazing out at the view, I move on to let the eager couple behind me take a photo (of the view, not of this sweaty woman glancing at her Garmin). The elevation begins to reverse until I'm pounding down the rocks at what feels like a dangerous speed. If I want to stop right now, it's tough – I'll go flying. Bear this in mind and please be careful.

Miraculously, I don't fall today.

Eventually, I emerge from the woodland to see a sign for the Offa's Dyke path, stretching for miles in the opposite direction to where I'm headed. Part of me is tempted to go and explore it, but also it's hot and I'm thirsty. If you do however want to explore more of the Offa's Dyke path, please bear in mind that it is actually 285km long, linking Sedbury Cliffs near Chepstow with the coastal town of Prestatyn on the shores of the Irish sea. It passes through no less than eight different counties and crosses the border between England and Wales over 20 times.

So, you know, not your average Saturday Parkrun. But there is an ultramarathon that takes place here: The Wild Horse 200. It's 200 miles across the trails and mountains of South Wales, along Offa's Dyke, traversing the Beacons Way before catching the Heart of Wales Line on to the Wales Coast Path and finish line at Worm's Head. Not for the faint-hearted, but a remarkable achievement for those who do it.

There are stunning views as I run above the river below. Great cliffs and glittering water give me a perfect excuse to sit on a nearby felled log and enjoy the view. I check my blood sugars. They are in range. This is always something to celebrate, no matter how many times I run.

I'm passed by many hikers and a few fellow runners, all of them smiling and all of them polite enough to greet me as I pass. I love it when I'm greeted by fellow runners and walkers. It doesn't always happen when running through busy towns and cities, but on the trails, everyone seems a little more relaxed and genuinely pleased to see someone else sharing their appreciation of the route.

The path is dry and dusty, sticking to my calves in fine golden layers. Bits of gravel shift just enough to keep me alert. I nearly go over a felled trunk and spend the next fifty metres pretending it didn't happen.

There are a lot of felled trunks here, which always makes me feel sad. Whenever I pass trees with small circles spray-painted on their trunks, I want to stop whoever is going to cut them down, even if I'm told it's necessary. Disease management, thinning, or conservation – I don't know what the reason is. But that doesn't stop the ache in my chest when I pass a once-living giant now cross-sectioned on the forest floor, its rings exposed.

The path merges back the way I came. I leave the felled trees behind and try to focus on the promise of a cold can of Pepsi Max.

*

If the ascent was tricky, then the descent is something of a challenge, too. I can't run most of it; there's far too great a risk of misjudging a step and flailing straight into a tree trunk. So, for the end of this run, I take it easy. Once more, I inhale the sweet garlic. But this time, I let the squealing little kids overtake me.

Once I'm back over the bridge, I know where I want to stop. The Anchor Inn is crowded today and I'm in the mood for something more relaxed and with more space for thinking. I head to the White Monk Tea Rooms.

It's not as chaotic here. There are plenty of seats outside, mercifully placed in the shade, and a sweet little gift shop where I seriously consider purchasing a Tintern Abbey magnet and a box of fudge. I check my blood sugars.

They are very good and I probably do not need fudge. Or another magnet.

After paying for my drink, I sit and let the condensation bead down the glass while I watch people mill around the Abbey across the road. A woman poses with a baby who refuses to stay still. A teenager tries to take a moody selfie. Someone is shouting in operatic bursts that echo off the Abbey walls.

It's all very alive and very human.

It's strange, sitting here now, knowing that I only have one more route left to show you. I've watched the seasons shift; watched a swell of leaves unlatching from the trees then burst back into life again. I've shivered in thermals and sweated in a vest. And, most importantly, *I've learned to read a map.*

Honestly, I can't wait to be asked for directions.

Llanrhidian

Location
Llanrhidian
SS 52669 95408

Distance
12K

Parking
Plenty of parking on Crofty Industrial Estate. I can't guarantee beauty before you hit the running path though, unless your aesthetic leans towards corrugated roofing and oil stains.

Facilities
The Welcome Inn is halfway through this run for a nice, icy glass of something soft and cold. Then you've got the Crofty Inn at the end for a celebratory pint and a home-cooked lunch.

Tips
PROMISE ME YOU'LL CHECK THE TIDE TIMES. Unless, of course, you fancy finishing this run somewhere off the coast of Burry Port, covered in weeds.

Llanrhidian

One of the things I've loved most about running the routes for this book is how they've pulled me into entirely new places – some by chance and many through generous recommendations from people who know their landscapes intimately. I've followed routes that mean something to others: the grief-paths, the training grounds, and the loops pounded into muscle memory. So it seems only fair to finish here, on a route that feels like it belongs to me, somehow.

This route smells of salt and cockles and whatever the tide coughed up that morning. The wind slants sideways over my face, bracingly fresh. It looks dramatically different each time I run it, depending on the tide, the season, the weather and time of day. And, I suppose, this is what keeps pulling me back here – the knowledge that every day, the water and the light will rush to greet me with something new.

I've mentioned Loughor Estuary a few times previously as the place where I first discovered my love of running. I now live on the other side of it, on what's often called "The Dark Side of Gower" (which, to be honest, is probably just snobbery but I've embraced it). This side, wild flat and exposed, is the side that's so often overlooked, yet deserves so much more attention. This might not look like the postcard-perfect South Gower with its dramatic seascapes exhaling gulls, miles of sprawling sand, and epic clifftops. But Llanrhidian Marsh is one of the best examples of a coastal saltmarsh in Britain, teeming with life and loved by birdwatchers. As an area of biodiversity, it's pretty damn important.

The route I'm running today is part of a Special Area of Conservation, a Special Protection Area and a Ramsar Site.[38]

There's even a chance of seeing the elusive otter and water vole, though I've not seen those yet. I have, however, witnessed Ted gently picking up a dying rat in his jaws, looking baffled, then putting it back down where he found it.

If you're driving here, I recommend parking on Crofty Industrial Estate, where you'll easily be able to join the Wales Coastal Path, signposted beside Jason's Garage. There's the 116 bus that also stops right outside the industrial estate, too.

The water is out right now, yet I can see the ghost of last night's high tide, all wrack and feathers, punctuated with broken cockle shells and clumps of wool. There's no one else out in the late morning sunshine, just the breeze bending ripples in the grass and the marsh glistening, becoming land again.

The path at the start of the run takes you straight onto the estuary and towards the point, where you can look across the water as far as Burry Port. Fun fact: on 18th June 1928, Amelia Earheart circled the Loughor estuary and just after 12.40pm touched down on the waters at Burry Port, becoming the first woman to ever fly across the Atlantic Ocean. "How lovely your country is," she'd apparently said after landing. "The stillness and the silence brings back again the almost awesome feeling which came to me as, hour after hour, we pushed forward through the thick clouds and fog. It was as if we were alone in the world. To think that 48 hours ago I was in America and now I am in Wales!"[39]

I return from the point and back onto the trail that hugs close to the fences of nearby buildings.

Ted's ears prick as the air rumbles with the sound of engines. Cockle pickers drag their trailers towards the water and I can smell the sharp stench of cockle shells, warm and rattling in the sun. I prise one from Ted's mouth, which he is furious about.

Cockles have been harvested from this estuary for centuries. It's one of several locations on this coastline where generations of hardworking women brought ashore cockles, using donkeys to transport the harvest. According to a 1916 report by the South Wales Sea Fisheries Association, it was estimated that nearly 320 tonnes of cockles were harvested monthly in the Penclawdd area. Every day, around 50 women would be seen bent over the sand, skirts hitched, hands raw, working the flats. And it really was brutal work. They'd then load the donkeys with up to 150kg of cockles and walk the 8 miles to Swansea Market to sell their haul.

Suddenly my 7am personal training sessions in a well-maintained gym don't seem all that bad.

Eventually, we reach the park where the road divides between the path up to the Crofty Inn (tempting) and the Marsh Road towards Llanrhidian. It's a weekday during school hours, so the swings are drained of squealing toddlers, hanging eerily still. The slide glints under the morning sun as if trying to remember the weight of a small body zipped up in nylon. A gull watches, swinging its yellow eye towards us from the climbing frame.

At high tide, this park is swallowed by the water, the swings skimming the surface. The slide plunges down into salt-grey. On more than one occasion, the tide has caught me out and I've had to detour back and onto the main road, adding half an hour to my 'quick morning walk'.

But not today.

I've checked the tide times. We are not about to get stranded. We have one final run to do.

*

The traffic is, fortunately, minimal this morning, which means we don't often have to perform a panicked leap into the hedgerow as a 4x4 barrels past with a boot full of wet spaniels. I clip Ted back onto his lead anyway (he has a habit of sauntering into the middle of the road like it's been laid out for him like a red carpet), and we drop to a more leisurely pace. We're not in a rush. Unless it's a lunch hour run, I'm almost never in a rush when I'm running.

If you want to see some of the best of Gower's wildlife, this place will spoil you. A buzzard carves lazy circles overhead. In the distance, curlews pick at the sand on elegant legs, their calls rising and falling in a slow, melodic whistle. If you're lucky, you might even spot an egret tiptoeing through the shallows, neck curved like a question mark, white feathers somehow immaculate despite the sludge. Or, if you're really lucky, a marsh harrier, soaring low and deliberate, scanning the reeds with its fierce little eyes.

In spring, everything here sharpens. The hedgerows fizzle into colour, every path edge dripping with bluebells, or more recently, buttery-yellow crocuses unfurling from slim stems. By high summer, even the muddiest path cracks underfoot. The grasses stand tall and vibrant green, buzzing with whatever's nesting or mating inside them (there's always something). You get the heat haze rising off the mudflats and the unmistakable perfume of sun-baked salt and horse-musk.

We're in the in-between stage of those seasons now. The bluebells are dying off, but the reeds are becoming thicker. Everything is so much greener than it's been for months.

It's not long before we realise we have company, and not in human form. Below a wizened tree that wouldn't look out of place on a Greek farm, ewes parade around the trunk with their lambs pressed close. I know these sheep well, so I don't panic. Unlike the sheep of previous chapters, they aren't going to chase me. One lamb performs what may be the single most adorable act I've witnessed on a run: it breaks rank, stomping clumsily across the path to follow a tabby cat that's just slinked across the road ahead of us. The cat doesn't even look back. Cats never care, really. The lamb, however, is convinced it has discovered something remarkable. It trots after it with clumsy determination, ears pricked, while its mother watches on as though she knows full well her child is a handful but trusts it to come back.

It's around this area that you'll notice curious stone structures and signs that read:

Llanrhidian

DANGER – Former Firing Range
Do not touch any military debris it may explode and kill
you. Telephone South Wales Police.

It's hardly 'Welcome to Gower', but it's still an important reminder of the history of this place. During the Second World War, this stretch of mud and estuary was a military training ground. Along this path, you'll spot what's left of a gunnery post, some barrack foundations, and a weather-worn lookout tower. The RAF used the marsh for air-to-ground target practice, and if you look closely, you can still make out two grassy mounds that once served as mock targets.

Today, these targets are surrounded by ponies. As we pass, a mare heaves, muscled and slow, raising her neck into a practised stretch. It's hard not to be inspired by these beautiful creatures I encounter every day:

> *The ponies sop to land's edges, eyes huge*
> *and tender, brown as cherry-pits. Churning*
> *wet marram, briny earth, currents*
> *bucking around them – the sound of something*
> *disappearing – as if the Earth were swallowing*
> *shock, alarmed at her own quick waters,*
> *cockles rattling her throat like pearls.* [40]

The mare pauses, head raised, nostrils flaring slightly at the scent of an overexcited Ted before deciding he's not worth the energy of even a snort.

★

We're at St David's Church now, a small but sturdy stone building overlooking the marsh. It opened on Easter Tuesday in 1898, with the Bishop of St David's in attendance. *The Cambrian* newspaper, never one to undersell a new build, called it a "very compact, well-finished little building", and commended it for saving locals from trudging to Llanrhidian or Penclawdd through weather better suited to sheep and sailors (or, of course, very strong women with very strong donkeys). By 2001, the church had reached the sort of age where refurbishment could no longer be put off. Fortunately, the community rallied and it was able to build a brand-new kitchen and toilet extension. If you don't think that's impressive, then you've clearly never tried hosting a bake sale or a harvest supper in a very old building without modern plumbing.

Over the years, St David's has earned its local nickname: *the little church on the marsh*, which sounds delightfully like something from a Thomas Hardy novel. And the reason it still stands here is because people know that places like this still matter to local communities.

As we run on, the landscape reveals more of itself. In the distance, the woodlands and sands of Llanmadoc stand dramatically against a clear sky. Houses give way to farmland, with rolling fields and a green tractor dozing at the edge, nose dipped in the grass, engine ticking with leftover heat. A light breeze rattles through barbed wire and the frail ribs of dying bluebells.

This final run has crept up on me, in a way. I didn't think much about what it would feel like to write the final one, in a place I know so well I could probably run it backwards (I don't plan on trying this, however). I thought maybe it would feel like just another route, another morning, another scribble in the notes app with sweaty thumbs and half-finished snatches of poetry. But now I'm here, it's like the full stop at the end of a story I didn't quite realise I was telling.

When I started this project, I thought I was just documenting trails: giving people a bit of route guidance, maybe a laugh or two, a list of where the decent coffee shops were hiding. What I didn't expect was how these runs would sneak into the deeper parts of my life, and how they'd become the place where everything else was allowed to unravel and, eventually, re-form.

Llanrhidian

I've learned that pace doesn't always matter, but noticing things does. That a run can be a way of listening, not just moving, and that solitude is often misunderstood. It doesn't always mean absence. Sometimes it simply means space. Space to think, to feel, to shift something in the body you didn't even realise was stuck.

Mostly, I've learned that you never really run the same path twice. The tides change. The light changes. And, over time, you change, too.

*

The marsh offers up slim rivulets of water, bottle-green ducks and the shells of crabs, suspended like ghosts in the long grass. Across the road, a man waves from his truck and I wave back.

We're coming close to our halfway pit stop. Now, you'll need to keep your wits about you here (especially if you tend to enter another world while listening to an absolute banger on your Spotify). There's a kissing gate that leads you into a winding country road without pavements. Go slow. Stay alert. And I don't care if you're just getting to a massive chorus on your favourite song; it's not worth ignoring your surroundings because you wanted to reach the epic guitar solo.

The hedgerows are thick with cow-parsley and the slow trails of pollinating bees. Approaching the end of this road, there's a sign that reads: *"CAUTION: Blind cat crossing."* Which, honestly, has always intrigued me.

I've still never seen the cat.

Now, if you really *want* to make the most of the benefits of hill training that I mentioned in a previous chapter, you've got an excellent opportunity here. As you run up to the Welcome Inn, there's a stretch of hill that extends all the way to the main road at a breathtaking incline. And by breathtaking, I mean you won't *actually* be able to breathe. It's steep.

I've tried it a few times, but I've never quite made it all the way to the top. I will one day, but not today. I'm ready for a glass of icy water and Ted is already straining towards a steel bowl with his tongue flapping.

I should probably mention an interesting but tragic speculation of a lost village not far from here. According to Reverend J.D. Davies of Llanmadoc and Cheriton, there was once a medieval village and church known as Llanellen, tucked somewhere off Welsh Moor, dating back to the reign of Edward VI. Aside from a memorial stone and a few scattered remains, there's nothing left. It's hard today to even imagine a whole community once stood there. Local folklore goes that a ship – returning from foreign waters – foundered in the Burry Estuary, and the survivors, drenched and desperate, dragged themselves up the hill towards Llanellen. The villagers welcomed them with generosity and open arms, entirely unaware that they were also welcoming in the plague.

Within a week, the entire village was said to be gone: either buried or vanished entirely.

Excavations ran from 1973 to 1985, with more research through the 1990s. What they found was intriguing: a two-chambered stone structure, likely a twelfth-century church built on top of an earlier timber one, plus the remains of a domestic building, 31 graves, and a collection of pottery, tools, and metal objects. At some point in the late thirteenth century, the church was converted into a farmhouse, and a second building was added. This might tell us people were living and working here well before the twelfth century, but it doesn't prove there was ever a full village as Davies claimed.

Still, there's no evidence that contradicts it either.

And then there's the whole issue of the plague. It's easy to be cynical about this kind of thing when it's presented as rural legend wrapped up in hindsight, but pottery found at the site dates to around 1350, which, inconveniently or not, lines up perfectly with the first arrival of the Black Death in Wales.[41]

Eventually, stone from the site was salvaged to build a bridge at nearby Wernffrwd. What wasn't taken is still said to be cursed. The legend insists that those who disturb the

Llanrhidian

remaining stones won't go unpunished, though it doesn't specify how.

I'm not going to test it.

If you're walking past Llanrhidian Church, take a moment at the gateposts. You'll find two memorial stones for Llanellen embedded there, unlabelled and easy to miss. Fortunately, next time you see it, you'll have plenty of folklore and speculation to bore your companions with, too.

★

The beer garden is almost empty and the heat is making me sleepy. It's Ted's lucky day today – the Welcome Inn serves doggy gelatos, which he is delighted about. As he slurps maniacally at the little blue tub, I sip iced water through a straw, relaxing my shoulders and breathing in the sticky afternoon air. Somewhere nearby, a lawnmower hums into life, a domestic interruption to the quiet. Once I've finished rehydrating, I trap a wasp under my glass and feel terrible about it, but not terrible enough to let it go to potentially sting my nose.

It's time to head back for our final return journey.

This time, as we jog through the marsh, the cows have muscled into the picture. They're hulking things, with gleaming red hides and eyes dark as plums. I scoop an overexcited Ted up in my arms and soothe him, walking past these magnificent beasts. I can't help but keeps imagining how it would feel for one to accidentally use me as a scratching-post or a human cushion.

Back through the farmland, there's the same tractor at the edge of the field, its body now casting a longer shadow. The sheep have shifted to a different patch of shade, and a single lamb watches us pass as if it might remember us from earlier. Its mother keeps it well within her sight.

There's something luxurious about the return stretch, when you're not trying to reach anything anymore. You're just going home to a cool shower, snacks, and comfier clothes.

The estuary is coming into view again. The tide has curled itself across the sand like an old blanket, spitting gulls into the landscape. Somewhere on the banks, a labrador shakes off its black fur, the water droplets sparkling in the sun. We slip off the marsh path and back onto the road, the Crofty Inn coming into view with its low white walls and hanging baskets just beginning to wilt in the heat. The pub hums with lunchtime chatter and the smell of frying bacon, but we're not stopping here today.

Ted trots beside me, tongue lolling, utterly content. Both of us are content.

You know, a good run will always do that to you.

Notes

1. Gower Management Association, *A History of St Illtyd's Church Oxwich*
2. Rees, Mark, *Paranormal Swansea and Gower*. Amberley Publishing (2024)
3. Gower Heritage Centre
4. Parc Le Breos
5. Natural Resources Wales
6. Oswald, F., Campbell, J., Williamson, C., Richards, J., & Kelly, P. (2020). *A Scoping Review of the Relationship between Running and Mental Health*. International Journal of Environmental Research and Public Health, 17(21), 8059
7. Cadw, Castell Coch
8. *Caerphilly Observer*
9. Caerphilly Golf Club
10. AllTrails, Caerphilly Mountain Circular
11. National Churches Trust, Margam Abbey
12. Morgan, A. (2021) 'She was as hard as Port Talbot Steelworks but dead soft underneath': A feminist autoethnography of life in 80s Port Talbot. In: Miskell, L. and Almond, G. (eds.) *Shaped by Steel: Landscapes, Lives and Legacies of a Global Industry*. Swansea: AHRC Social Worlds of Steel project, pp. 47–48
13. National Churches Trust, Beulah Chapel, *Margam*
14. Parks and Gardens: *Brombil* (www.parksandgardens.org/places/brombil)
15. Adidas, 2023
16. www.whiteribbon.org.uk/about-us
17. Cadw
18. Visit Wales: *Merthyr Mawr Warren National Nature Reserve*
19. lonelygoat.com, *80/20 Training* (July 2020)
20. Walters, R., & Hefferon, K. (2020). 'Strength becomes her'— Resistance training as a route to positive body image in women. *Qualitative Research in Sport, Exercise and Health*, 12(3), 446–464
21. 'Tell it to the Trees', *Little Universe* (Parthian, 2024)
22. Delia Jay and Rosemary Lewis (2008). *St Mary The Virgin Church, and hill fort at Caerau*

23. CAER Heritage Project, Heart of Cardiff Heritage Trails, *Red Trail III Caerau Hill Fort*
24. Atlas Obscura, *Maen Ceti* [Arthur's Stone]
25. Swansea University. (2021). *Arthur's Stone, Gower.* Ancient World
26. Cadw, *Weobley Castle*
27. Morris, Jan, *The Matter of Wales: Epic Views of a Small Country* (1984)
28. Llantwit Major History Society
29. Lambert, Jonathan and Mark, *The Lost Mansions of Llantwit Major*, Glamorgan History and Archaeology (2020)
30. UWC Atlantic
31. Visit the Vale, *Nash Point Beach and Lighthouse* (2021)
32. Plough and Harrow, Monknash
33. Alderman, B., Olson, R., Brush, C. et al. *MAP training: combining meditation and aerobic exercise reduces depression and rumination while enhancing synchronized brain activity.* Translational Psychiatry 6, e726 (2016)
34. Mipham, S. (2012). *Running with the Mind of Meditation: Lessons for Training Body and Mind.* Harmony Books
35. Cadw, *Tintern Abbey*
36. Natural Resources Wales, *Wyndcliff Wood, near Chepstow*
37. Barnes, Hopkins, McGuigan, Kilding: 'Effects of different uphill interval training programs on running economy and performance', International Journal of Sports Physiology (2013, Mar 26.)
38. Gower National Landscape
39. Carradice, Phil, BBC. 2010. 'Amelia Earhart Flies the Atlantic.' *BBC Wales History*, May 13, 2010
40. Holborow. N, *Shore Mares,* Arachne Press (2025). *Afonydd: Poems for Welsh Rivers / Cerddi Afonydd Cymru* | 50 poems and their translations in an entirely bilingual Welsh/English anthology in praise of Welsh rivers.
41. *Hauntings of Wales*, The Paranormal Information and Learning Centre (2006)

Acknowledgements

Wild Running wouldn't possibly be the book it is now without the help and support of the below. I'm so grateful to all of you.

My *Wild Running* companions, Inês, Ian, Matt, The Doc, Bronwen (also the star CEO behind Seren who first gave me the space to tell this story - thank you so much) and, of course, Ted the Dog.

My incredible editor Rebecca F John. I was already a massive fan of your work and to be able to work with you on this was a dream. Thank you for making the process so much easier than I expected and for your excellent suggestions and kindness. To Bronwen, Simon, Jamie, Sarah and everyone at Seren who made it such a joy to work with you.

The super-talented photographer Ceri, who climbed even higher hills than I did to get the best photographs. You've smashed it and you're amazing.

My Salty Poets Mari, Emily, Rae, Rhys, Adam and Alan for always providing the best, most honest feedback and keeping my passion for writing alive. You're all legends.

My dear friends Roisin, Zoe, Chelsey and Ali who cheered me on all the way through when I succumbed to inevitable self-doubt. Your support absolutely kept me going. Thank you for putting up with my moments of panic and for understanding why I sometimes said no to ten tequilas because I had a 5am run planned the next day somewhere off the M4.

To the Running Punks for your enthusiasm and support. You're the best running community there is.

To Phil at Strength Lab for consistently providing excellent strength training and getting me to hit PRs. I've probably saved a good few injuries thanks to you. To Fran (fellow running enthusiast), Jackie, Dave and Savannah for being the best training partners.

To my beautiful family for cheering me on at both writing and running events over the years. I love you millions.

And finally, to all the wild runners out there. I hope these routes bring you as much joy as they brought me (when I wasn't lost up a hill in the arse end of nowhere).

About the Author

Natalie Ann Holborow is a winner of the Terry Hetherington Award and the Robin Reeves Award, a runner-up of the Rheidol Prize for Fiction and shortlistee of the Bridport Prize and Cursed Murphy Spoken Word Award. Her writing residencies with the British Council, Literature Wales and Kultivera have seen her writing and performing poetry in Wales, Ireland, Sweden and India. She is the author of the poetry collections *And Suddenly You Find Yourself*, *Small* and *Little Universe*, which was shortlisted for Wales Book of the Year 2025, and has featured on BBC Radio 4's The Verb.

Wild Running is her first book of non-fiction.

About the Author's Dog

This is Ted, my running buddy and self-appointed route director. His approach to trail running is largely interpretive. While I focus on the stuff that would make great writing later, Ted's busy propelling himself after squirrels, rolling through anything remotely disgusting and leading us down paths I'm 90% sure aren't public rights of way. Without Ted, *Wild Running* would have been a lot shorter and much less fun.

(This photograph was taken a mere two minutes after we'd given him a bath.)